*It's Easier
than you Think*

It's Easier than You Think

Jo Seagar

Photography by Jae Frew

RANDOM HOUSE
NEW ZEALAND

A RANDOM HOUSE BOOK published by Random House New Zealand
18 Poland Road, Glenfield, Auckland, New Zealand

For more information about our titles go to www.randomhouse.co.nz
A catalogue record for this book is available from the National Library
of New Zealand

Random House New Zealand is part of the Random House Group
New York   London   Sydney   Auckland   Delhi   Johannesburg

First published 2010

© 2010 recipes Jo Seagar, photographs Jae Frew

The moral rights of the author have been asserted

ISBN 978 1 86979 420 0

Design: Kate Barraclough and Jae Frew
Printed in China by Everbest Printing Co Ltd

To my wonderful husband Rosso
for better
for worse
and for lunch

For Emily's two
great kids, Liam and Grace

Sharing our passion for good food is what the Cook School is all about, here, at Seagars in Oxford, North Canterbury

A wonderful meal experience can be created with a few ingredients and doesn't have to be difficult. It is an act of love, cooking for people you care about, but that doesn't have to equate to a long complicated recipe that goes over the page with lists of unfamiliar ingredients and highly complicated techniques and explanations of how it all works. I just love it when students exclaim, 'Oh my goodness, it's easier than you think!'

We try to keep our recipes and methods short and 'un-fussy', and with resulting meals that really call in the compliments.

Loads of supermarkets and gourmet delis stock an ever-increasing range of really good, quality ingredients and useful items to assist the cook. Pasta sauces, spice pastes and roasted peppers, among others, are the kind of shortcut products that, together with a few fresh ingredients, make it easy to create an impressive dish that will have them singing your culinary praises and requesting second servings.

The food is simple, old fashioned and up to date. Homely, with a certain style — just right for a casual modern dining experience. It's easy to prepare, easy to eat and kind of familiar to everyone.

And good food makes both the cook and the guests happy!

Emily Cross has been my very capable assistant in the Cook School for three years now and I know I just couldn't have managed without her.

This book is very much her baby, too. We have worked together, refining, testing and improving our collection of recipes, all ones that we use with great success in our cooking classes.

New development is always exciting and we work through ideas from the drawing board — in our case, scraps of paper and jotted down notes or lists of key ingredients — to test runs where we always have lots of staff hovering around ready 'to help' taste-test the results.

We run classes for children and young adults (definitely Emily's forte), Gluten-Free classes, also something that Emily specialises in, through to our Lunch & Learn one-day programme and two-day residential Cook Class/Getaway weekend packages.

Emily is a country girl, Canterbury born and bred. She shares my philosophy of simple generous entertaining. She is as passionate as I am about good food. We work together as a team.

Emily trained as a chef and professional cookery tutor in Christchurch. I'm just going to unashamedly skite a little here on your behalf Em! Top student of her class and New Zealand Apprentice of the Year!

She has travelled and worked overseas as a pastry chef and tutored in different cook schools and polytechs around the globe and still continues with a one-day-a-week tutoring position at the Christchurch Polytechnic Institute of Technology, as well as working for Seagars. At the same time, she's raising two great children, Liam and Grace!

This is our first book together and we are already buzzing with ideas for more. Emily will be joining me at Seagars Cook School in Umbria, Italy, this year and I'm sure that it will inspire us both immensely: we can't wait!!

Honey Toasted Muesli • Banana Berry Smoothie • Full English Breakfast Frittata • Cinnamon French Toast • Buttermilk Waffles with Banana & Maple Syrup • Ham, Cheese & Tomato Baked Eggs • Breakfast Pancakes • Oaty Apple Pancakes •

Banana Yoghurt Muffin Loaves • Lemon Cream-cheese Frosting • Savoury Scramblers • Eggs Benedict • Blender Hollandaise • Eggs Cooked in Onion Rings

Honey Toasted Muesli

Serves 12 / makes 10 cups

¼ cup	runny honey
¼ cup	oil (rice bran or canola)
3 cups	rolled oats
1 cup	flaked almonds
1 cup	Brazil nuts
1 cup	pumpkin seeds
1½ cups	sunflower seeds
¼ cup	sesame seeds
¼ cup	flax seeds
1 cup	coconut
1 cup	bran
2 cups	dried fruit — cranberries, currants, raisins, etc

Preheat the oven to 160°C. Line a large roasting dish with non-stick baking paper.

In a small saucepan melt the honey with the oil, whisking to combine.

Place the rolled oats, almonds, Brazil nuts and seeds in the prepared roasting dish. Drizzle the melted honey and oil over, and mix well.

Bake for 20–25 minutes, stirring a couple of times, until the mixture is lightly browned and toasted. Allow to cool slightly, then mix in the coconut, bran and dried fruit.

Cool completely, then store in an airtight container.

Serve with fresh fruit, milk and/or yoghurt.

The pace of change in the world
is so fast, people like to cling
to the familiar.

Banana Berry
Smoothie

Serves 4

2	ripe bananas
1 cup	raspberries, fresh or frozen
3 cups	low-fat milk, well chilled
½ cup	yoghurt, plain or berry flavoured
1 teaspoon	vanilla
1 tablespoon	runny honey
2–3	ice cubes

Place all the ingredients in a blender and blend until smooth and frothy.

Serve immediately in tall glasses.

Variation — the berries can be replaced with tinned pears or peaches, or fresh kiwifruit.

If you have an ovenproof non-stick frypan — one that has a handle that can go in the oven — you can add the egg mixture to the frypan and bake the frittata in the pan. Remember the handle will heat up in the oven, so make sure you use gloves when removing the pan.

Full English
Breakfast Frittata

This is a great way of cooking everybody's favourite breakfast foods together in one easy dish. Bacon, eggs, mushrooms, cheese, potatoes, tomatoes and sausages — and of course tomato sauce on the side.

Serves 4–6

10	eggs
1 cup	sour cream
	salt and freshly ground black pepper
2 tablespoons	oil
6	rashers rindless bacon
2 cups	sliced button mushrooms
6	sausages, cooked and sliced
6 small	potatoes, cooked and cut into cubes
12	cherry tomatoes, halved
1 cup	grated cheese
	toast and tomato sauce to serve

Preheat the oven to 180°C. Coat a lasagne or small roasting dish with non-stick baking spray.

Beat the eggs and sour cream together in a bowl, and season with the salt and pepper.

Heat a non-stick frypan to medium-high, add the oil and cook the bacon and mushrooms until the bacon starts to crisp. Then add the sliced sausages and cubed potato, and stir-fry for a couple of minutes. Tip the mixture into the prepared dish. Add the halved cherry tomatoes and grated cheese. Pour in the egg and cream mixture and lightly mix through.

Bake until the egg is set and slightly puffed up (15–20 minutes). Cut into big slices and serve with toast and tomato sauce.

Cinnamon
French Toast

Serves 4

4	eggs
1½ cups	milk (I prefer full-cream milk for this recipe)
¼ cup	caster sugar
1 teaspoon	ground cinnamon
8 thick slices	French stick
50 g	butter
	icing sugar to dust
	maple syrup to serve

Whisk together the eggs, milk, caster sugar and cinnamon. Place the bread slices in a shallow dish and pour the egg mixture over. Turn the bread, letting it soak for a few minutes.

Heat a large non-stick frypan over a medium-high heat and melt half the butter. When the butter is sizzling, add half the soaked bread slices and cook until golden brown. Then turn and cook the other side. Remove from the pan and keep warm. Wipe the pan and start again with the remaining butter and bread slices.

Serve on warm plates with a dusting of icing sugar and a little jug of maple syrup. This recipe is lovely with fresh fruit and crispy bacon.

Brunch is a classic way to entertain family and friends, probably because it accommodates so many tastes and ages.

Buttermilk Waffles
with Banana & Maple Syrup

This is a really good mixture for waffles that are light and fluffy but crisp on the outside. The buttermilk, which is available in the dairy section of the supermarket, is the secret ingredient.

Makes 6–8 waffles

2¼ cups	flour
2½ teaspoons	baking powder
¼ teaspoon	salt
3	eggs, separated
¼ cup	caster sugar
1½ cups	buttermilk
2 tablespoons	runny honey
125 g	butter, melted
	sliced banana to serve
	maple syrup to serve

Heat the waffle irons.

Mix the flour, baking powder and salt together in a bowl.

Beat the egg yolks and caster sugar together in a separate bowl until thick. Stir in the buttermilk, honey and melted butter. Then slowly pour the buttermilk mixture into the dry ingredients, mixing to a smooth batter. Whisk the egg whites until stiff peaks form, then fold gently into the waffle batter.

Lightly coat the hot waffle iron with non-stick baking spray. Pour about ½ cup of the mixture into the waffle iron and cook until golden brown. Remove and keep warm. Repeat with the remaining mixture.

Serve with sliced banana and a drizzle of maple syrup. Crispy bacon is also a perfect accompaniment.

Ham, Cheese & Tomato
Baked Eggs

Serves 4

½ cup	chopped ham
2	spring onions, thinly sliced
1	tomato, chopped
4	eggs
4 tablespoons	cream
	salt and freshly ground black pepper
½ cup	grated cheese
	toast soldiers to serve

Preheat the oven to 180°C. Coat 4 individual ½ cup-sized ovenproof dishes with non-stick baking spray.

Divide the ham, spring onions and tomato evenly between the dishes. Break an egg into each dish and let it sit on top of the ham mixture. Spoon 1 tablespoon of cream into each dish over the egg and season with salt and pepper. Sprinkle the top with grated cheese.

Place the dishes on an oven tray and bake for 8–10 minutes until the eggs are just cooked.

Serve with toast soldiers.

Breakfast
Pancakes

Makes 8–10

3	eggs
½ cup	caster sugar
1½ cups	self-raising flour
30 g	butter, melted
¾ cup	milk
1 teaspoon	vanilla
	fruit to serve
	maple syrup to serve

Beat the eggs and caster sugar together until light and fluffy. Gently mix in all the other ingredients until the batter is smooth and quite thick. Allow to stand for 10 minutes before cooking.

Heat a non-stick frypan to medium, then lightly coat with non-stick baking spray. Ladle several large spoonfuls of the batter into the pan and cook until golden brown on both sides, turning once when bubbles appear on the surface. Remove from the pan and keep warm. Repeat with the remaining mixture.

Serve with fruit and a drizzle of maple syrup and/or whipped cream.

Variations
— serve with chocolate, caramel or strawberry sauce, or lemon juice and caster sugar.
— fresh or frozen blueberries can be added to the pancakes when cooking.

CREAMOATA

GUARANTEED 3¼ lbs.

SERGEANT DAN'S
FAVOURITE BREAKFAST

THE NATIONAL BREAKFAST

NET WEIGHT 3 LBS. 4 OZS.

5 lbs. net.

CORN-VITA
WHEATMEAL

PREPARED BY
W.E. COOK & COY
CHRISTCHURCH, N·Z·

Oaty Apple
Pancakes

Makes 8–10

1 cup	rolled oats
1 cup	milk
2	eggs, beaten
¾ cup	self-raising flour
¼ cup	sugar
½ teaspoon	salt
25 g	butter, melted
½ cup	tinned or stewed apple
	maple or golden syrup to serve
	fresh fruit to serve
	icing sugar to dust (optional)

Put the oats in a bowl, cover with the milk and leave to stand for 5 minutes to soften.

Add the remaining ingredients, gently stirring until well combined.

Heat a non-stick frypan to medium and coat with non-stick baking spray. Place heaped spoonfuls of the batter into the pan and cook until golden brown on both sides, turning once when bubbles appear on the surface. Remove from the pan and keep warm. Repeat with the remaining mixture.

Serve with maple or golden syrup, fresh fruit, or dust with icing sugar if using.

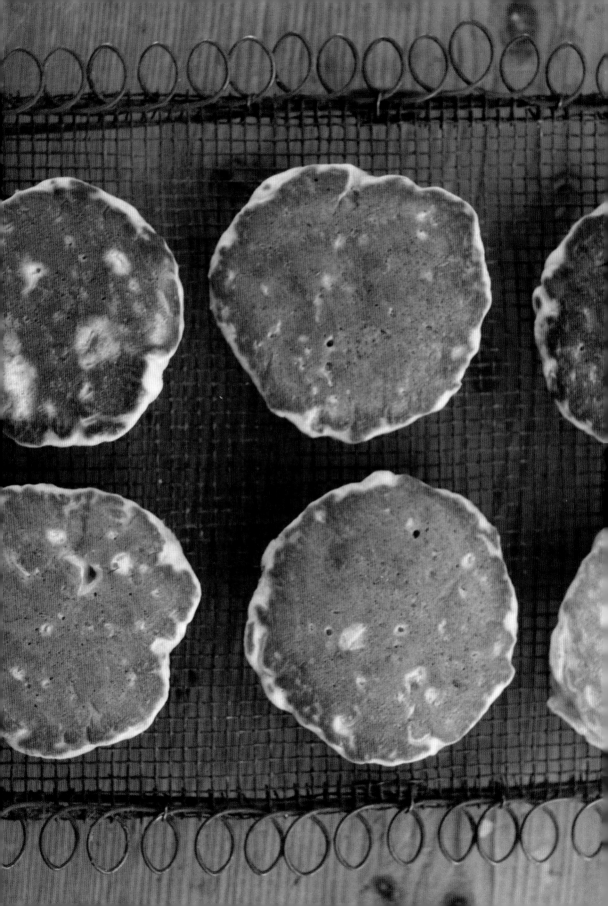

Banana Yoghurt
Muffin Loaves

Makes 12

1 cup	sugar
100 g	butter, melted
3	eggs
2	bananas, mashed with a fork
1 teaspoon	baking soda
½ cup	milk, warmed
150 ml	yoghurt, plain or fruit flavoured
2 cups	self-raising flour

Preheat the oven to 180°C. Coat a 12-cup small loaf or muffin tray with non-stick baking spray. Be generous with the spray in the cavities of the tins.

Mix the sugar, melted butter, eggs and mashed banana together in a large bowl. Stir the baking soda and warm milk together in a separate bowl, then pour into the banana mixture. Add the yoghurt and flour, mixing lightly to just combine. Do not overmix or the loaves will be quite tough. Spoon into the prepared tins.

Bake for 25–30 minutes until browned. Cool in the tins for 5 minutes then turn out on a wire rack to cool completely.

They can be served plain or iced with lemon cream-cheese frosting (see recipe on page 44) when cold.

If you have too many bananas ripening at the same time, put some in the freezer until you need to use them — for this recipe or for a cake.

Lemon Cream-cheese
Frosting

Makes enough for 12 muffins

125 g	regular cream cheese, softened to room temperature
	grated rind and juice of 1 lemon
2 cups	icing sugar

Whisk the cream cheese, lemon rind and juice
together to a smooth and soft consistency.
Then beat in the icing sugar until well
combined and there are no lumps. The mixture
should be thick, like frosting. If you use an
extra-large lemon you may need a little more
icing sugar to achieve the right consistency.

Spread over cold banana yoghurt muffin loaves.

It is best to use regular cream cheese for the frosting
as it is firmer and holds its shape better than low-fat
varieties.

Do fewer things better.
Cook a few things and buy others.
There's no prize for exhausting
yourself and having expectations
that are too high. Play to your
strengths.

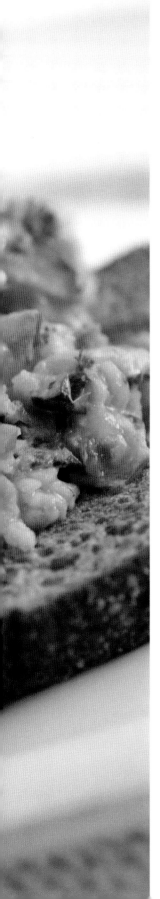

Savoury Scramblers

4	eggs
	salt and freshly ground black pepper
25 g	butter
4	button mushrooms, sliced
1	tomato, chopped
1	spring onion, thinly sliced
1 tablespoon	chopped parsley
1 tablespoon	cream
¼ cup	grated tasty cheese
2 slices	toast to serve

Whisk the eggs with the salt and pepper in a bowl.

Melt the butter in a frypan and fry the mushrooms over a medium heat until lightly browned. Then stir in the tomato, spring onion and parsley. Pour in the egg mixture and gently stir until the eggs are lightly set. Add the cream and cheese, mixing until combined. Remove from the heat and serve on freshly made toast.

Variation — ham, bacon, spinach, peppers or cooked potato can be added instead of or in addition to the mushrooms, spring onion and tomato.

Eggs Benedict

4	rashers rindless streaky bacon
4	eggs
2	English muffins, split in half
4 tablespoons	hollandaise sauce (see recipe on page 53)

In a non-stick frypan, fry the bacon over a high heat until crispy.

To poach the eggs, bring 5–6 cm of water to the boil in a frypan or small saucepan. Swirl the water with a slotted spoon and crack the eggs into the water. Turn down the heat so the water is just gently bubbling. After 3–4 minutes remove the eggs with a slotted spoon and drain on paper towels.

Toast the muffins and gently re-heat the hollandaise.

Divide the bacon between the toasted muffin halves, carefully top each with a poached egg and spoon the hollandaise sauce over.

Variation — ham, tomato, spinach or smoked salmon can be used instead of bacon.

Blender
Hollandaise

This recipe makes enough for 20 Eggs Benedict because hollandaise
is difficult to make in small volumes. It can be gently rewarmed when
needed.

4	egg yolks
1 tablespoon	lemon juice
1 tablespoon	white wine vinegar
	salt and freshly ground black pepper
200 g	hot melted butter
100 g	extremely soft butter (the consistency it would be if it had been sitting in the sun)

Place the egg yolks in a blender or food processor, and with the machine
running slowly add the lemon juice, white wine vinegar and salt and
pepper. Blend until the yolks are light, pale and creamy. Slowly drizzle in
the hot melted butter through the funnel, then add the softened butter
to the mix. Taste and add extra salt and pepper if required.

Store in the fridge for a week to 10 days.

Eggs Cooked in
Onion Rings

These are great for keeping fried eggs in a neat
little package when cooking a lot at one time,
for, say, a Sunday-morning brunch party. Make
as many as you require.

1   onion ring per person
1   egg per person

Peel a large onion and cut into slices 1.5–2 cm
thick.

Place the onion slices on top of a silicone
sheet on the barbecue or in a non-stick frypan
heated to medium. Break an egg into each ring
and cook for 4–5 minutes until set. Cover the
pan with a lid, or close the barbecue lid to help
cook the tops nicely.

Carefully remove with a fish slice.

Either fry the other bits and pieces of the
onion or use it in another recipe. Onion also
freezes well.

Valencia Orange Salad • Sweetcorn, Courgette & Mint Fritters • Asparagus Soup with Lemon & Lime Crème Fraîche • Broccoli & Cauliflower Cheese Gratin • Spanakopita • Dijon Tomato Tarts • Bacon, Cheese & Parsley Savouries • Cheese & Ham Pinwheels • Spinach & Bacon Wraps • Blue Cheese & Button Mushroom Bites • Curried Parsnip Chowder • Whitebait Fritters in a

Mouthful • Prawn Quesadillas • Butternut Pumpkin & Coconut Soup • Salmon & Dill Frittata • Olive & Pepper Parcels • Spring Onion Flatbreads • Parsnip & Carrot Mash with Toasted Cumin Seeds & Cashews • Feta, Courgette & Caper One-pan Pie • Boiled New Potatoes with Honey Mint Dressing • Beetroot, Apple & Orange Salad • Pistachio, Parsley & Orzo Salad

Valencia
Orange Salad

4 handfuls	baby spinach leaves, washed and trimmed
4	oranges
½ cup	orange marmalade
2 tablespoons	white wine vinegar
½ cup	olive oil
1 teaspoon	Dijon mustard
½ cup	orange juice
	salt and freshly ground black pepper
½ cup	sliced almonds

Arrange the spinach leaves on a serving platter. Grate the rind of 2 of the oranges over the spinach. Peel and segment all 4 oranges, removing any pith, and arrange the segments over the spinach.

In a blender, place the marmalade, vinegar, olive oil, mustard, orange juice, and salt and pepper. Blend well to a smooth consistency.

To serve, drizzle the dressing over the salad, then top with a sprinkling of sliced almonds.

Sweetcorn, Courgette
& Mint Fritters

Serves 4 / makes 8 fritters

1 cup	milk
2	eggs
1½ cups	self-raising flour
1 cup	sweetcorn (frozen, fresh or canned)
2 small	courgettes, grated
2 tablespoons	chopped fresh mint leaves
2 tablespoons	sweet chilli sauce
	salt and freshly ground black pepper
	oil for frying
½ cup	sour cream to serve
	extra sweet chilli sauce to serve

Whisk the milk and eggs together in a large bowl. Then mix in the flour, sweetcorn, courgette, mint and sweet chilli sauce, and season generously with salt and pepper.

Add enough oil to cover the base of a large non-stick frypan and heat to medium-high. Keep the pan at this temperature so the fritters don't brown too quickly before the centres are cooked. For each fritter, pour about ¼ cup of mixture into the frypan and cook until golden brown. Turn and cook the other side. Keep the fritters warm while you cook the remaining mixture.

Serve with a dollop of sour cream and sweet chilli sauce.

Asparagus Soup with
Lemon & Lime Crème Fraîche

Serves 4–6

50 g	butter
1 cup	sliced shallots
2 cloves	garlic, crushed
2 large bunches (about 1 kg)	asparagus, trimmed and roughly chopped, reserving tips for garnish
2 teaspoons	ground coriander
1 litre	chicken or vegetable stock
	milk if needed
	salt and freshly ground black pepper
½ cup	crème fraîche
	grated rind of 1 lemon
	grated rind of 1 lime
½ teaspoon	lemon juice
½ teaspoon	lime juice

Melt the butter in a large saucepan over a medium heat. Add the shallots and garlic and cook for 4–5 minutes, stirring often.

Add the asparagus and coriander to the pan and pour in the stock. Bring to the boil and simmer until the asparagus is tender (7–8 minutes).

Purée the soup in batches in a blender, returning it to the saucepan. Add a little milk if the soup is too thick and season generously with salt and pepper. Add the reserved asparagus tips and gently reheat.

Mix the crème fraîche with the lemon and lime rind and juice.

Divide the soup between serving bowls. Top with a dollop of the lemon and lime crème fraîche mixture and garnish with remaining asparagus tips.

I like to serve at least some hot food when entertaining. Cold food can feel like lukewarm hospitality.

Broccoli &
Cauliflower Cheese Gratin

Serves 4

1 head	broccoli, cut into florets
½ small (about 500 g)	cauliflower, cut into florets
250 g	sour cream
1 cup	grated cheese
2 tablespoons	chopped parsley
	salt and freshly ground black pepper
	extra grated cheese to sprinkle

Preheat the oven grill. Coat an ovenproof dish, or 4 individual dishes, with non-stick baking spray.

Steam or microwave the broccoli and cauliflower until just tender (6–7 minutes).

Mix the sour cream, grated cheese and parsley together in a bowl. Season with salt and a generous amount of pepper. Place the vegetables in the prepared dish or dishes. Spoon the sour cream and cheese mixture over, and sprinkle with extra cheese. Grill until golden brown.

 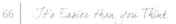

Spanakopita

Greece's Famous Spinach & Feta Filo Pie

Serves 6–8

1 bag	baby spinach leaves or 3 bunches spinach, washed and trimmed
1 tablespoon	olive oil
1	onion, peeled and finely sliced
3 cloves	garlic, crushed
4	eggs
400 g	feta cheese, crumbled or chopped
1 cup	cooked rice (you can use brown rice)
2 tablespoons	chopped fresh dill, or 2 teaspoons dried dill
	salt and freshly ground black pepper
16 sheets	filo pastry, covered with a damp tea towel until required to prevent drying out
200 g	butter, melted
	lemon wedges to serve

Preheat the oven to 180°C. Coat a 20 x 30 cm sponge-roll tin or ovenproof dish with non-stick baking spray.

Steam or microwave the spinach until just wilted. Drain and squeeze out any water. Coarsely chop the leaves and place in a large bowl.

Heat the olive oil to medium in a frypan and cook the onion and garlic until softened, but not browned. Add to the spinach and mix in the eggs, feta, rice and dill. Season with just a little salt, remembering that feta is quite a salty cheese, and lots of pepper.

Brush 1 sheet of filo with melted butter. Repeat until you have 8 sheets layered flat, on top of each other. Fold the layered sheets in half and use these to line the base of the prepared tin. Spoon the spinach mixture on to the filo. Butter and layer the remaining filo. Fold the layered sheets in half and place on top of the spinach mixture. Ensure the top is well buttered. I score the pastry into portion sizes with a sharp knife so the pie is easier to slice when cooked.

Bake for 25–30 minutes until golden brown and crispy. Cool for 5 minutes in the tin before cutting into pieces. Serve with lemon wedges.

Dijon Tomato Tarts

Serves 6

2–3 sheets	*frozen flaky or puff pastry, thawed*
2 tablespoons	*Dijon mustard*
10–12 small	*tomatoes, thinly sliced*
1	*egg yolk, beaten with 2 teaspoons water*
	flaky salt and freshly ground black pepper
	extra-virgin olive oil to drizzle
50 g	*Parmesan, shaved with a potato peeler*
	rocket or flat-leaf parsley to garnish (optional)

Preheat the oven to 200°C. Coat a baking tray with non-stick baking spray.

Cut out pastry circles 10–12 cm in diameter and place on the prepared tray. (I use a small saucer or noodle bowl as a stencil.) Spread a little Dijon mustard on to each pastry round, leaving a 1 cm edge all the way around. Arrange the tomato slices on top of the mustard in an overlapping circle with the end slice positioned in the centre. Brush the edges with the egg wash. Season generously with salt and pepper. Then drizzle with a little extra-virgin olive oil and place the shaved Parmesan on top.

Bake for 18–20 minutes until golden and puffed.

These tarts can be served hot or cold, and perhaps garnished with a few rocket or flat-leaf parsley leaves.

Bacon, Cheese
& Parsley Savouries

Makes 24

3 sheets	frozen puff pastry, thawed
2 cups	grated cheese
4 rashers	rindless streaky bacon, chopped into small pieces
2	eggs
¾ cup	cream
2 tablespoons	chopped parsley
	salt and freshly ground black pepper

Preheat the oven to 180°C. Coat 2 trays of 12 tartlet tins with non-stick baking spray.

Using a 5 cm cookie cutter, press out 24 circles of pastry and line the prepared tartlet tins. Sprinkle equal amounts of cheese into each case and divide the bacon between them.

Beat the eggs, cream, parsley and salt and pepper together in a bowl. Pour the mixture into a small jug, then fill each tartlet case three-quarters full.

Bake for 15–20 minutes until puffed and golden. Twist the savouries to loosen them from the tins and cool on a wire rack.

Serve warm or reheat later. These savouries freeze well.

Cheese & Ham
Pinwheels

Makes 36–40

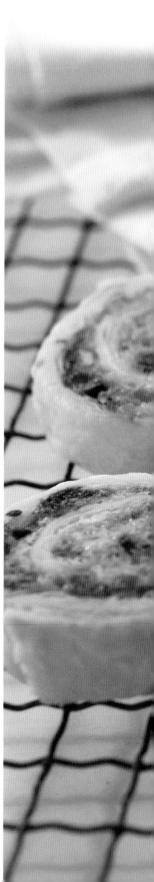

3 sheets	frozen puff pastry, thawed
1	small egg, beaten
1 cup	diced or chopped ham
1 cup	grated cheese
2	spring onions, finely sliced
	garlic salt to sprinkle

Preheat the oven to 200°C. Coat a baking tray with non-stick baking spray.

Place the pastry sheets on a flat surface and brush them lightly with the beaten egg. Scatter equal amounts of the ham, cheese and spring onion over the top of each sheet, leaving a 1 cm edge at the top of the longest side.

Sprinkle each sheet with garlic salt and roll up tightly, sealing the ends by crimping with a fork. Cut into slices around 1 cm thick and place on the prepared tray.

Bake for 10 minutes, then turn the pinwheels and bake for another 4–5 minutes until crisp and well puffed.

Serve warm.

Spinach & Bacon Wraps

Serves 4

4	flour tortillas (I like to use wholemeal tortillas)
4 tablespoons	cream cheese (you can use a low-fat or softened variety)
4 tablespoons	snipped chives or parsley
½	lemon
8 rashers	rindless streaky bacon, cooked until crisp
4 handfuls	baby spinach leaves, washed and trimmed
	salt and freshly ground black pepper

Place the tortillas on a flat surface and spread with cream cheese. Sprinkle the chives over and then squeeze over a splash of lemon juice. Crumble the bacon into bits and divide evenly between the tortillas. Scatter the spinach leaves over, and season with salt and pepper.

Roll up tightly, folding in the ends, and cut each wrap in half to serve.

Clever

Clever ingredients
          with little handling
produce big results.

Blue Cheese &
Button Mushroom Bites

Makes 24

1 cup	sliced button mushrooms
150 g	blue cheese
5	eggs
	salt and freshly ground black pepper
1 tablespoon	self-raising flour

Preheat the oven to 200°C. Coat a 24-cup mini-muffin tray with non-stick baking spray.

Divide the sliced mushrooms between the mini-muffin cups. Then crumble the blue cheese over the mushrooms.

Whisk the eggs, salt, pepper and self-raising flour together in a bowl until combined. Transfer the egg mixture to a small jug, then pour over the mushrooms and blue cheese, filling to just below the top of each muffin cup.

Bake for 7–8 minutes until puffed, lightly golden brown and just set.

Serve warm.

Curried Parsnip
Chowder

Serves 4–6

3	parsnips, peeled and finely chopped
2	onions, peeled and chopped
50 g	butter
1 tablespoon	mild curry powder
1 litre	vegetable stock
	salt and freshly ground black pepper
1 cup	cream or milk (more if needed)
½ cup	chopped parsley
	oil for deep-frying
2	extra parsnips, peeled and topped and tailed
	olive oil to serve

Heat a medium-large saucepan to medium and put in the parsnips, onions, butter and curry powder. Cook, stirring, for 10 minutes until soft. Don't have the heat too high — you just want to soften, not brown, the vegetables. Add the stock and season with salt and pepper. Bring to the boil and simmer for about 20 minutes, stirring occasionally.

Transfer to a food processor or blender and blend with the cream or milk to a thick and creamy consistency. You may need extra cream or milk to get the desired consistency. Return the soup to the saucepan and gently reheat, stirring in the parsley.

To make the parsnip ribbons, heat the oil to 180°C in a deep-fryer.

Slice off ribbons of parsnip using a vegetable peeler.

Fry the ribbons until crispy — this only takes 30–40 seconds. Be careful as they can burn easily. Drain on paper towels.

Garnish the soup, if desired, with the deep-fried parsnip ribbons and a drizzle of olive oil.

Whitebait Fritters
in a Mouthful

Makes 24

6	eggs
1 teaspoon	salt
1 teaspoon	lemon pepper or lime kelp seasoning
	freshly ground black pepper
2 tablespoons	self-raising flour
1 tablespoon	finely chopped parsley
200 g	whitebait

Preheat the oven to 200°C. Coat a 24-cup mini-muffin tray with non-stick baking spray.

In a bowl, whisk together the eggs, salt, lemon pepper or lime kelp seasoning and black pepper. Then add the flour and parsley and continue to whisk until combined. Transfer the mixture to a jug.

Divide the whitebait evenly between the mini-muffin cups. Pour the egg mixture over the whitebait, filling each cup to three-quarters full.

Bake for 8–10 minutes until puffed and the egg has set. The fritters should be a light golden brown.

Serve immediately while fresh and warm.

Variation — this is a great base recipe. For the whitebait you can substitute little prawns, chopped mussels, chopped scallops or smoked salmon. For a gluten-free option, replace the self-raising flour with a gluten-free version.

The new silicone and metal FlexiPro muffin tins are extremely good for this recipe as the fritters turn out so easily.

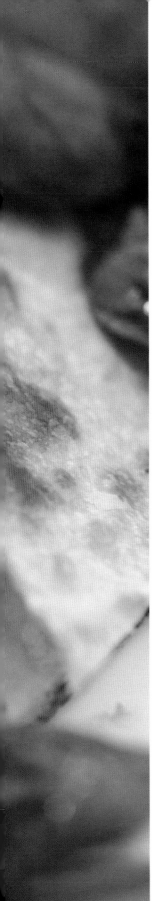

Prawn Quesadillas

Makes 4

	olive-oil spray
8 x 20 cm	flour tortillas
250 g tub	store-bought hummus
1 cup	cooked peeled prawns, chopped
2 tablespoons	sweet chilli sauce
1 cup	grated tasty cheese
2 large handfuls	baby salad leaves to serve

Coat a large frypan with olive-oil spray and heat to medium.

Lay 4 tortillas on a flat surface and spread with the hummus. Sprinkle with equal amounts of the chopped prawns, then drizzle the sweet chilli sauce over and top with the grated cheese. Press a plain tortilla down firmly on top of each filled tortilla.

Slip 1 quesadilla into the hot pan and cook for 2–3 minutes. Then flip over to cook the other side. Remove from the pan and keep warm. Repeat with the remaining quesadillas.

Cut each quesadilla into wedges and serve with baby salad leaves on the side.

I find kitchen scissors best for cutting the quesadillas.

Butternut Pumpkin
& Coconut Soup

Serves 4

½	butternut pumpkin, peeled, deseeded and chopped to make about 3 cups
1	onion, peeled and chopped
2 cloves	garlic, crushed
1	walnut-sized piece fresh ginger, peeled and finely chopped or grated
½ cup	desiccated coconut
1 litre	vegetable or chicken stock
1 can (about 2 cups)	coconut cream
	salt and freshly ground black pepper to taste

Place the pumpkin, onion, garlic, ginger, coconut and stock in a saucepan. Bring to the boil then simmer, with the lid on, until the pumpkin is tender (about 3 minutes).

Purée the soup in batches with the coconut cream in a blender or food processor. Season with salt and pepper. If the soup is too thick it can be thinned down with extra coconut cream or milk. Check the temperature of the soup and return to the heat if necessary.

Variation — coconut milk is thinned-down coconut cream, which you can use as a substitute if you like. Similarly, a reduced-fat evaporated milk with coconut flavouring can be used, which will make a very low-fat version of this soup.

Sunday Supper revisited!

Salmon & Dill
Frittata

Serves 4

1 tablespoon	oil (rice bran or canola)
2	leeks, thinly sliced and well washed
200–300 g	hot-smoked salmon, flaked
8	eggs
2 tablespoons	chopped fresh dill
	salt and freshly ground black pepper
½ cup	grated tasty cheese
2 large handfuls	baby salad leaves to serve

Preheat the oven to 190°C.

Heat the oil to medium in a medium-sized non-stick ovenproof frypan. Add the leeks and cook for 7–8 minutes until soft, stirring occasionally. You want to soften, not brown, the leeks. Place the salmon over the top of the leeks.

Beat the eggs, dill, and salt and pepper together in a bowl. Then pour the mixture over the salmon and leeks, giving it a little stir to mix the eggs through. Sprinkle with the grated cheese.

Place the pan in the oven and bake for 25–30 minutes until the frittata is puffed up and set in the middle. The cheese should be lightly brown on top.

Remove the frypan from the oven, remembering the handle will be hot. Carefully lift the frittata out of the pan on to a chopping board.

Slice and serve with a few salad leaves on the side.

If your frypan is not ovenproof, you can transfer the softened leeks to a cake tin that has been coated with non-stick baking spray. Then continue with the method above.

Olive & Pepper
Parcels

Serves 4

2 medium-large	red peppers
½ cup	pitted olives, chopped
1 medium	courgette, grated
½ cup	grated cheese
1 cup	chopped cherry tomatoes
2	spring onions, sliced
	salt and freshly ground black pepper
2 large handfuls	baby salad leaves to serve

Preheat the oven to 180°C.

Slice the peppers in half through the stalk, remove the seeds and lay flat, open side up, in a roasting dish. Cut a little slice off the underneath of the peppers, pan side down, to make sure they sit flat.

Mix the olives, courgette, cheese, tomatoes and spring onions together in a bowl. Season with salt and pepper. Spoon the mixture into the pepper halves, pressing it down to ensure it is firmly packed.

Bake for 25–30 minutes. The peppers should still be quite firm but the filling melted and browned on top.

Serve for lunch or as a first course with a few salad leaves.

Spring Onion Flatbreads

Great to accompany a barbecue or to use as a wrap.

Makes 12

2 cups	flour
1 tablespoon	oil (rice bran or canola)
250 ml	boiling water
4 tablespoons	sesame oil
3	spring onions (green part only), finely sliced

Place all the ingredients in a food processor and process to form a dough. With floured hands, flatten the dough into a disc and wrap in plastic wrap. Chill in the fridge for 30 minutes.

With floured hands, divide the dough into 12 equal portions. Pat or roll out each ball into thin flatbreads or pancakes. You can also use a pasta machine to thinly and evenly roll out the dough.

Heat a large non-stick frypan to medium-high and spray with a little oil. Fry each flatbread for 1 minute on each side until golden. Keep them warm under a clean tea towel.

These flatbreads can also be cooked on a barbecue flat plate. I use a silicone sheet to prevent the flatbreads sticking.

Sourcing local produce is a very desirable and noble notion on the one hand, but on the other, I'm very grateful we live in the age of airfreight and extensive culinary to-ing and fro-ing, so that we can enjoy all sorts of foody imports year-round.

It might be great living in a farmers' market district in sunny California where you can enjoy gorgeous different things to eat every month of the year. But for us in the heart of North Canterbury winter – I'd be rather tired of Brussels sprouts and boiled tubers by the time spring time arrived.

Parsnip & Carrot Mash
with Toasted Cumin Seeds & Cashews

Serves 4

3 large	parsnips, peeled and sliced
4 large	carrots, peeled and sliced
½ teaspoon	salt
2 tablespoons	oil (rice bran or canola)
½ cup	cashew nuts
1 teaspoon	cumin seeds
pinch	salt
25–50 g	butter
½ teaspoon	extra salt
	freshly ground black pepper

Place the parsnips and carrots in a saucepan and cover with cold water. Add the first ½ teaspoon of salt, bring to the boil and simmer until very tender.

While the parsnips and carrots are cooking, heat a frypan to medium. Add the oil, cashew nuts and cumin seeds. Cook the nuts and seeds for a couple of minutes until golden brown, stirring constantly. Remove from the pan and drain on paper towels. Season with a pinch of salt.

When the parsnips and carrots are cooked, drain well and return to the pot. Add the butter, the second ½ teaspoon of salt and the pepper, and mash well.

Serve in a bowl with the cashews and cumin seeds sprinkled over the top.

'Like your mother made' — only better.
With the appeal of nostalgia,
this indulges the palate and the eye.

Feta, Courgette &
Caper One-pan Pie

Serves 4–6

2 tablespoons	olive oil
3	courgettes, thinly sliced
1 clove	garlic, crushed
2 tablespoons	chopped parsley
3 tablespoons	drained capers
6	eggs, lightly beaten
2 tablespoons	milk
	salt and freshly ground black pepper
100 g	feta, cut into cubes
	tomato chutney or relish to serve

Preheat the oven grill to high.

Heat the oil to medium-high in a non-stick ovenproof frypan and sauté
the courgettes until tender. Add the garlic, parsley and capers and mix
thoroughly.

Whisk the beaten eggs, milk, and salt and pepper together in a bowl.
Pour the egg mixture into the pan, stirring it in quickly, then add the
feta. Press the mixture down firmly in the pan.

Place the frypan under the grill for 4–5 minutes until the egg is firm and
set, and the top is nicely golden brown.

Serve with tomato chutney or relish, and a green salad.

Boiled New Potatoes
with Honey Mint Dressing

Serves 4

2 teaspoons	salt
1 kg	baby new potatoes (I love Jersey Bennes in season), washed and scraped

For the dressing

1 cup	fresh mint leaves
1 tablespoon	runny honey
2 tablespoons	white wine vinegar
2 teaspoons	Dijon mustard
	salt and freshly ground black pepper
1 cup	oil (rice bran or canola)

Bring a large saucepan of salted water to the boil. Rinse the potatoes well and place in the boiling water. Simmer gently until they are just tender (about 15 minutes). Drain well.

To make the dressing, place all the ingredients in a blender and process until well combined. The dressing will keep in the fridge for around a week.

To serve, drizzle the potatoes with the honey mint dressing. This dish can be served either warm or cold.

Beetroot, Apple
& Orange Salad

Serves 4

6	fresh medium-sized beetroot, skins on
3	apples, peeled, cored and cut into wedges
2	oranges
¼ cup	fresh mint leaves, finely sliced

For the dressing

½ cup	light olive oil
2 tablespoons	cider vinegar
1 teaspoon	wholegrain mustard
¼ teaspoon	salt
	freshly ground black pepper

Wash the beetroot and place in a saucepan.
Cover with cold water and bring to the boil.
Simmer for 1 hour, or until easily pierced
with a knife. Allow the beetroot to cool in the
saucepan, then drain and slip the skins off
by rubbing them with your fingers. Cut the
beetroot into wedges and place in a bowl with
the apple wedges.

Grate the rind of the oranges over the beetroot
and apple. Peel and segment the oranges,
removing any pith, and add to the beetroot and
apples along with the mint. Mix together well.

To make the dressing, place the ingredients in a
blender and blend until well combined.

To serve, drizzle the dressing over the salad and
gently toss to combine.

*Variation — if you don't have fresh beetroot, this
recipe works well with tinned baby beetroot.*

Pistachio, Parsley & Orzo Salad

Serves 4

2 tablespoons	salt
2 cups	orzo pasta
1 cup	shelled pistachio nuts
1 cup	chopped parsley
2 tablespoons	olive oil
	grated rind and juice of 2 lemons
	salt and freshly ground black pepper

Bring a large saucepan of water to the boil. Add the salt and pasta, and boil until the pasta is tender (7–8 minutes). Drain and rinse the pasta in cold water to wash off the salty water. Leave to cool.

When the pasta is cold, place it in a bowl with the pistachios, parsley, olive oil, and lemon rind and juice, and toss well. Season with salt and pepper.

Vanilla Cupcakes • Raspberry Fudge Brownie • Easy Parmesan Bread • Mixed-in-the-saucepan ANZAC Biscuits • Cheesy Scones • White Chocolate & Cherry Oat Biscuits • Ham, Cheese & Pineapple Muffins • Butterfly Cakes • Caramel Oat Slice • Prize-winning Gluten-free Sponge Cake • Easy Peasy Crunchy Peanut Butter Biscuits •

Raspberry, White Chocolate & Coconut Friands • Gingersnaps • Mini Yo-yos • Lemon Syrup Buttermilk Cake • Chocolate Caramel Slice • Feijoa Poppyseed Muffins • Chickpea, Pumpkin & Sunflower Seed Loaf • 'Thank You' Chocolate Gift Cakes • Chocolate Orange Biscuits

Old fashioned
yet strangely up to date.

Vanilla Cupcakes

Makes 12

125 g	butter
¾ cup	caster sugar
1 teaspoon	vanilla
2	eggs
1½ cups	self-raising flour
½ teaspoon	baking powder
1 tablespoon	sour cream
½ cup	milk
For the vanilla frosting	
250 g	butter, softened
3 cups	icing sugar, sifted (more if needed)
1–2 tablespoons	boiling water
1 teaspoon	vanilla
	food colouring (optional)

Preheat the oven to 180°C. Line a 12-cup muffin tray with paper cases and lightly coat with non-stick baking spray.

Beat the butter, sugar and vanilla until pale and creamy. Add the eggs one at a time, beating well after each addition. Stir in the remaining ingredients and mix until smooth. Spoon the mixture into the cases.

Bake for 15 minutes. Remove the cupcakes from the tray in their paper cases and cool on a wire rack. Allow to cool completely before icing.

To make the icing, beat the butter until light and creamy. Gradually mix in the icing sugar and boiling water until the mixture is light and smooth. The frosting should be a fluffy consistency — you may need to use extra icing sugar. Stir in the vanilla and food colouring if using.

Ice the cooled cupcakes with the vanilla frosting and decorate as desired. They will keep in an airtight container for 3 days.

Raspberry Fudge Brownie

300 g	butter, cut into cubes
300 g	dark chocolate, roughly chopped
6	eggs
2 cups	caster sugar
1½ cups	flour
½ cup	baking cocoa
2 teaspoons	vanilla
1 cup	whole raspberries (fresh or frozen)
½ cup	extra chopped chocolate

Preheat the oven to 170°C. Line a 25 x 35 cm sponge-roll tin with non-stick baking paper.

Gently melt the butter and chocolate together in a large microwave-proof bowl in the microwave, or gently heat over a saucepan of simmering water, stirring until blended.

Beat the eggs and caster sugar until pale and creamy, then add the melted butter and chocolate. Sift the flour and cocoa together and add to the mixture with the vanilla. Mix until well combined. Pour into the prepared tin and sprinkle with the raspberries and extra chopped chocolate.

Bake for 25–30 minutes. Cool in the tin and cut into slices when cold. Store in an airtight container for up to 5 days, or freeze.

A packet of chocolate melts is 375 g. Grab a handful for the extra 1/2 cup for sprinkling and use the remaining 300 g in the brownie.

'Only generous people make good bread' – old proverb

Easy Parmesan Bread

5 cups	high-grade flour
1½ cups	grated Parmesan
1 teaspoon	salt
1 teaspoon	dried mixed herbs — oregano, thyme and marjoram
1 tablespoon	dried yeast
½ teaspoon	sugar
2½ cups	warm (bath temperature) water
	extra grated Parmesan to sprinkle

Coat a 20 x 30 cm sponge-roll tin with non-stick baking spray.

Place the flour, Parmesan, salt, mixed herbs, yeast, sugar and warm water in the large bowl of a cake mixer or in a food processor. Mix or process until well combined and a soft sticky dough forms.

Transfer the dough into the prepared tin, spreading it out evenly. Sprinkle with the extra Parmesan and leave in a warm place — the window-sill or hot-water cupboard — until the dough has risen to twice its size (about 30 minutes). Meanwhile, preheat the oven to 200°C.

Bake for 15–18 minutes until golden brown. Remove the bread from the tin and cool on a wire rack.

Mixed-in-the-saucepan
ANZAC Biscuits

Makes 26–28

125 g	butter
2 tablespoons	cold water
2 tablespoons	golden syrup
1 teaspoon	baking soda
1 cup	rolled oats
1 cup	long-thread coconut
1 cup	flour
1 cup	brown sugar

Preheat the oven to 160°C. Line 2 oven trays with non-stick baking paper.

Put the butter, cold water and golden syrup in a medium to large saucepan over a moderate heat and melt the butter, almost bringing the mixture to the boil. Add the baking soda and remove from the heat. Mix in the dry ingredients until well combined.

Roll the mixture into small walnut-sized balls and place on the prepared trays. Press flat with a fork, allowing a little room between each for the biscuits to spread.

Bake for 15–18 minutes. Allow to cool on the trays for 5 minutes before transferring to a wire rack to cool completely. These will keep in an airtight container for 2–3 weeks.

Cheesy Scones

Makes 10–12

3 cups	self-raising flour
½ teaspoon	salt
1 cup	grated tasty cheese
1 cup	milk
25 g	butter
	extra milk to brush

Preheat the oven to 200°C. Coat an oven tray with non-stick baking spray.

Place the flour, salt and cheese in a large bowl. Heat the milk and butter together in the microwave, or in a small saucepan, until the butter has melted. Pour the wet ingredients into the dry ingredients and mix to form a soft moist dough. A little extra cold milk may be required to get the dough to the right consistency.

Dust the bench with flour and tip out the dough. Press out to a 3 cm thickness and cut out the scones, either in squares or with a round cookie cutter, and place on the prepared tray. I like soft-sided scones so I place mine close together so they touch when they rise in the oven.

Brush the tops with milk, add grated cheese and bake for 12–15 minutes until golden brown and cooked through. Cool on a wire rack, covering with a clean tea towel to keep them soft and moist.

Serve warm with butter. These scones keep well and can be reheated in a microwave to freshen them up.

White Chocolate &
Cherry Oat Biscuits

Makes 30

250 g	butter
¾ cup	sugar
3 tablespoons	sweetened condensed milk
½ teaspoon	vanilla
1½ cups	rolled oats (I use wholegrain rolled oats)
1½ cups	flour
1 teaspoon	baking powder
1 cup (250 g)	white chocolate, chopped
150 g	(about 1 cup) glacé cherries, chopped

Preheat the oven to 170°C. Coat 2 oven trays with non-stick baking spray and line with non-stick baking paper.

Beat the butter and sugar until creamy. Then add the condensed milk and beat until pale and smooth. Stir in the vanilla, rolled oats, flour and baking powder, then add the chopped white chocolate and cherries.

Place spoonfuls of the mixture on the prepared trays and press flat with a wet fork.

Bake for 25–30 minutes until golden brown. Allow to cool for 2–3 minutes on the trays, then transfer to a wire rack to cool completely. These will keep in an airtight container for 10 days to 2 weeks.

Using a tube of condensed milk makes handling small measurements a lot easier.

Delicious biscuits that make you feel like a kid again.

Ham, Cheese & Pineapple Muffins

Makes 12

2 cups	flour
4 teaspoons	baking powder
1 cup	grated tasty cheese
1 cup	crushed pineapple, drained
½ cup	chopped lean ham
½ teaspoon	salt
2 tablespoons	chopped parsley
¼ cup	oil (rice bran or canola)
1	egg
1¼ cups	milk

Preheat the oven to 180°C. Coat a 12-cup muffin tray with non-stick baking spray.

Place all the ingredients in a large bowl and gently mix until just combined. Don't overmix or the muffins will be heavy and solid — light muffins only need a light mixing. Spoon the mixture into the prepared muffin cups.

Bake for 25–30 minutes until puffed up and golden brown. Cool for 5 minutes in the tins, then tip out on a wire rack to cool completely.

Butterfly Cakes

Makes 12

100 g	*butter*, softened
½ cup	caster sugar
2	eggs
1 teaspoon	vanilla
1 cup	self-raising flour
2 tablespoons	cornflour
For the filling	
150 ml	cream
¼ teaspoon	vanilla
1 tablespoon	icing sugar
	raspberry jam
	extra icing sugar to dust
	fresh raspberries to garnish

Preheat the oven to 180°C. Line a 12-cup muffin tray with paper cases and lightly coat with non-stick baking spray.

Beat the butter and sugar together in a large bowl until light and fluffy. Then add the eggs one at a time, stirring between each addition. Add all the remaining ingredients and mix together well. Spoon the mixture into the prepared cases to just over half full.

Bake for 12–15 minutes until risen and lightly golden. Remove the cakes from the tray in their paper cases and cool on a wire rack.

To make the filling, whip the cream with the vanilla and icing sugar until it holds its shape.

Using a small sharp knife, cut a round the size of a $2 coin out of the tops of the cakes and cut each round in half. Spoon raspberry jam and whipped cream into each hole and arrange the half rounds on an angle to make butterfly wings. Dust with icing sugar and garnish with fresh raspberries if desired before serving.

Confidence

Cooking is about developing an understanding of food. A sense of confidence and assurance in the kitchen and simply the desire to make something absolutely delicious for friends to eat.

They'll be fighting over who
is cleaning up – licking
the bowl, that is!

Caramel Oat Slice

This really delicious treat is very much for special occasions only.
Makes a large slice — 20–24 pieces

2 cups	flour
1 cup	self-raising flour
1 cup	desiccated coconut
2 cups	brown sugar
3 cups	rolled oats
2	eggs
300 g	butter, melted
For the filling	
200 g	butter
2 x 400 g cans	sweetened condensed milk
4 tablespoons	golden syrup
1 teaspoon	vanilla
½ cup	dark and white chocolate melts, melted, to decorate (optional)

Preheat the oven to 180°C. Line a large 25 x 35 cm slice or sponge-roll tin with non-stick baking paper, making sure the paper has a good overhang, and coat with non-stick baking spray.

Combine the dry ingredients in a bowl. Then add the eggs and the melted butter, mixing well. Press two-thirds of the mixture into the tin.

To make the filling, gently melt the butter, condensed milk and golden syrup together. Mix until well blended, then add the vanilla. Pour over the base and sprinkle the remaining crumbly mixture on top.

Bake for 30 minutes. Cool in the tin and refrigerate. To get beautiful slices, it's best to leave it until the next day to cut it.

If decorating, drizzle with melted dark and white chocolate before serving. This slice will keep in an airtight container for 7–10 days.

Prize-winning Gluten-free
Sponge Cake

1 cup	sugar
3 tablespoons	water
4	eggs, separated
½ teaspoon	vanilla
1½	cups cornflour (make sure it is not wheaten cornflour)
1 teaspoon	gluten-free baking powder
½ teaspoon	salt
	whipped cream to fill
	peaches or strawberries to fill
	icing sugar to dust

Preheat the oven to 180°C. Coat 2 shallow 21 cm sponge tins with non-stick baking spray and line the bases with non-stick baking paper.

Place the sugar and water in a microwave-proof bowl or a small saucepan and bring to the boil in the microwave or on the stovetop.

Beat the egg whites with an electric mixer until stiff. Slowly drizzle in the hot sugar and water mixture while the mixer is still running. Then beat really hard. Mix in the egg yolks and vanilla. Sift the dry ingredients, then carefully fold them in to the egg mixture — be very gentle with the folding process. Carefully pour the sponge mixture into the prepared tins.

Bake for 18–20 minutes. As soon as you remove the sponges from the oven, drop the tins from knee height, square on to the floor — no kidding! This is an odd, but tried-and-true, sponge-making trick that 'shocks' the cake and stops it deflating.

Sandwich the two sponges together with the whipped cream and fruit. Dust the top with icing sugar. Cut into wedges with a serrated knife.

'Child's play' but 'adult joy'

Easy Peasy Crunchy
Peanut Butter Biscuits
(gluten-free)

Makes 24

2 cups	crunchy peanut butter
2 cups	caster sugar
2	eggs

Preheat the oven to 170°C. *160* Line a baking tray with baking paper and coat with non-stick baking spray.

Place all the ingredients in a bowl and mix until well combined. Spoon teaspoonfuls of the mixture on to the prepared tray. Flatten each with a wet fork, leaving room between them for spreading.

Bake for 15–20 minutes or until light golden brown. Remove from the tray to cool completely on a wire rack. These will keep in an airtight container for 5–10 days.

Raspberry, White Chocolate & Coconut
Friands (gluten-free)

Makes 12 or 24 mini-muffin-sized friands

100 g	butter
100 g	white chocolate melts
1¼ cups	desiccated coconut
1 cup	icing sugar
½ cup	gluten-free flour mix
7	egg whites, very lightly beaten
½ teaspoon	raspberry essence (optional)
1 cup	raspberries (fresh or frozen)
	icing sugar to dust

Preheat the oven to 180°C. Coat friand moulds or a 24-cup mini-muffin tray with non-stick baking spray.

Gently melt the butter and white chocolate melts together in a microwave-proof bowl on medium in the microwave. Place all the remaining ingredients, except the raspberries, together with the melted butter and chocolate in a large bowl and mix until just combined.

Transfer the mixture to a jug and pour into the friand moulds or mini-muffin tray until just over half full. Top each with 2–3 raspberries — 1 if using a mini-muffin tray. There is no need to thaw the frozen raspberries.

Bake for 20–25 minutes — 12–15 minutes if using the mini-muffin tray — until golden brown. Remove from the oven and allow to cool for 5 minutes before turning out to cool completely on a wire rack.

To serve, dust with icing sugar. Freshly cooked and still warm friands are delicious but they also reheat well.

Gingersnaps

Makes 40

125 g	butter, softened
¾ cup	brown sugar
½ cup	golden syrup
2 cups	flour
2 tablespoons	ground ginger
½ teaspoon	baking soda

Preheat the oven to 180°C. Line 2 oven trays with non-stick baking paper.

Beat the butter and brown sugar until light and fluffy. Stir in the golden syrup until well blended. Then mix in the flour, ginger and baking soda until well combined.

With floured hands, roll the mixture into small, golf-ball-sized balls. Place on the prepared trays, allowing room between each one for spreading. Do not flatten as the biscuits do this themselves, forming the traditional cracked top of gingersnaps.

Bake for 15–20 minutes until golden brown. Cool on a wire rack. These will keep in an airtight container for 2–3 weeks.

Mini
Yo-yos

Makes 24

180 g	butter, softened to room temperature
¾ cup	icing sugar
1 teaspoon	vanilla
½ cup	custard powder
1 teaspoon	baking powder
1½ cups	flour
For the lemon butter icing	
2 tablespoons	lemon juice
1 tablespoon	butter, melted
1 teaspoon	grated lemon rind
2 cups	icing sugar
1 tablespoon	custard powder

Preheat the oven to 160°C. Line 2 oven trays with non-stick baking paper.

Place all the ingredients in a food processor or the bowl of a cake mixer and mix until well combined. With floured hands, roll the mixture into small balls. If the mixture is too soft to handle, cool it in the fridge for 10 minutes, then try again. Place on the prepared trays and press flat with a wet fork.

Bake for 18–20 minutes until very lightly golden and quite firm, but not browned. Cool on a wire rack.

To make the icing, mix the lemon juice and butter together. Then add the lemon rind, icing sugar and custard powder, beating to a thick, smooth consistency.

Once the biscuits are cold, join pairs together with the icing. This can be piped or spread on to the biscuits. These will keep in an airtight container for up to 2 weeks.

Love one another and be happy.
It's as simple and as
difficult as that.

Lemon Syrup Buttermilk Cake

Serves 8–10

200 g	butter, softened
1½ cups	caster sugar
3	eggs
	grated rind of 2 lemons
¼ cup	lemon juice
¾ cup	buttermilk
2 cups	self-raising flour

For the lemon syrup

	grated rind of 2 lemons
¼ cup	lemon juice
¼ cup	water
½ cup	caster sugar
	softly whipped cream or thick yoghurt to serve

Preheat the oven to 180°C. Coat a 23 cm Bundt cake tin with non-stick baking spray — be generous so it gets into all the indentations.

Beat the butter and sugar until light and fluffy. Add the eggs, one at a time, beating well after each addition. Add the lemon rind and juice, buttermilk and flour, and mix together well. Pour into the prepared tin.

Bake for 45–50 minutes or until a skewer inserted in the centre of the cake comes out clean. It will pull away from the edges of the tin as well. Cool in the tin for 5 minutes, then carefully invert on a wire rack. Clean the tin and immediately return the cake to the tin while it is still warm.

To make the syrup, put all the ingredients in a small saucepan over a medium heat and stir until the sugar has dissolved. Bring to the boil and boil for 3–4 minutes. Pour over the warm cake and cool in the tin.

Turn the cooled cake out on to a plate and serve with softly whipped cream or thick yoghurt.

Variation — you can substitute limes or oranges for the lemon.

Laughter

It is around the table that friends
understand best the warmth
of being together.

Here's a toast to love and laughter
and happily ever after.

Chocolate Caramel
Slice (gluten-free)

Makes 20 pieces

1½ cups	gluten-free flour mix
¾ cup	brown sugar
¾ cup	desiccated coconut
180 g	butter, melted
For the caramel	
70 g	butter
2 tablespoons	golden syrup
400 g can	sweetened condensed milk
For the chocolate topping	
140 g	chocolate
70 g	butter

Preheat the oven to 180°C. Line a 20 x 30 cm slice tin with non-stick baking paper and coat with non-stick baking spray.

To make the base, combine the flour, sugar and coconut in a bowl. Then mix in the butter until just combined and press into the prepared tin. Bake for 10–15 minutes or until lightly golden brown.

To make the caramel, melt the butter in a saucepan over a low heat, then mix in the golden syrup and condensed milk. Stir until the mixture has thickened and is a pale caramel colour. Pour over the cooked base. Bake for 15 minutes or until an even golden colour. Allow to cool.

To make the topping, gently melt the chocolate and butter together in a microwave-proof bowl in the microwave, or gently heat over a saucepan of simmering water, stirring until well blended. Spread the topping over the cooled caramel and allow the chocolate to set.

Remove from the tin and place on a board to cut into pieces. This slice will keep in an airtight container.

Feijoa Poppyseed
Muffins

Makes 12

125 g	butter, softened
¾ cup	brown sugar
2	eggs
5	feijoas, insides scooped out and mashed with a fork
	grated rind and juice of 1 lemon
¼ cup	milk
1¾ cups	self-raising flour
½ teaspoon	mixed spice
2 tablespoons	poppy seeds

Preheat the oven to 180°C. Coat a 12-cup muffin tray with non-stick baking spray.

Beat the butter and sugar together in a large bowl until light and fluffy. Add the eggs one at a time, stirring between each addition. Stir in the mashed feijoas, lemon rind and juice, and milk. Mix in the flour, mixed spice and poppyseeds until just combined. Spoon the mixture into the prepared muffin tray.

Bake for 15–20 minutes until lightly browned.

Handy tip — if the mixture starts to curdle, or go lumpy, when adding the eggs, stir in a tablespoon of self-raising flour.

Add lemon juice to the mashed feijoas to stop them from going brown.

New Zealand cooks are not bound
by culture or tradition.

Chickpea, Pumpkin & Sunflower Seed Loaf

Makes 16–18 slices

300 g	pumpkin, peeled and chopped into small pieces
400 g can	chickpeas, drained and rinsed
2	eggs
¼ cup	oil (rice bran or canola)
½ cup	milk
½ cup	bran
1¾ cups	self-raising flour
1 teaspoon	baking powder
½ teaspoon	salt
½ teaspoon	ground white pepper
1 teaspoon	ground cinnamon
1 tablespoon	sunflower seeds

Preheat the oven to 180°C. Coat a 12 x 22 x 7 cm loaf tin with non-stick baking spray and line with non-stick baking paper.

Place the pumpkin pieces in a microwave-proof bowl and cook on high for 6–8 minutes until soft. Transfer to a food processor with the chickpeas and process to a smooth consistency. Add the eggs, oil and milk and mix well. Then add the bran, flour, baking powder, salt, white pepper and cinnamon. Pulse until well combined, scraping down the sides of the bowl. Spoon into the prepared loaf tin and sprinkle the top with sunflower seeds.

Bake for 50–55 minutes or until a skewer inserted in the centre of the loaf comes out clean.

Cool for 5–10 minutes in the tin, then turn out on a wire rack to cool completely before slicing. This loaf will keep in an airtight container for 5–7 days.

The 10 cm square cake tins or little square cake tin trays are available from specialty cookware stores.

'Thank You'
Chocolate Gift Cakes

Makes 3 x 10 cm square cakes or 12 small square cakes

125 g	butter
½ cup	golden syrup
3	eggs
1 cup	milk
1 cup	caster sugar
2 cups	flour
¼ cup	cocoa
2 teaspoons	baking powder
2 teaspoons	baking soda
375 g	dark chocolate melts
200 ml	cream
½ cup	melted white chocolate
½ cup	melted dark chocolate

Preheat the oven to 180°C. Coat 3 x 10 cm square cake tins or a tray of 12 individual square cake tins with non-stick baking spray.

Melt the butter in a large bowl in the microwave. Stir in the golden syrup until well blended. Add the eggs, milk and sugar and beat until well combined. Mix in the flour, cocoa, baking powder and baking soda. Pour into the tins. Bake for 15–20 minutes until a skewer inserted in the centre of each cake comes out clean. Cool for 3 minutes, then carefully turn out on a wire rack to cool.

Gently heat the chocolate melts and cream together in the microwave on high for 25 seconds. Stir and repeat until the mixture is the consistency of a thick sauce. Cool for 10 minutes then spread over the cake tops and sides.

Drizzle a sheet of non-stick baking paper with the melted white chocolate. Then drizzle the dark chocolate over. When set, cut or break into sections and place around the cakes, tying on with a ribbon so the cakes look like wrapped-up parcels. Garnish further if desired.

Chocolate Orange
Biscuits

Makes 24

75 g	butter, softened
½ cup	brown sugar
½ cup	caster sugar
	grated rind of 1 orange
1	egg
½ cup	chocolate chips
½ cup	rolled oats
½ teaspoon	baking soda
1 cup	flour
1 cup	dark chocolate melts to decorate

Preheat the oven to 180°C. Line a baking tray with non-stick baking paper and coat the paper with non-stick baking spray.

Mix all the ingredients in a large bowl. Spoon walnut-sized balls of the mixture on to the prepared tray and flatten with your finger, leaving plenty of room between each for spreading.

Bake for 10–12 minutes. Cool on the tray for 5 minutes, then transfer to a wire rack to cool completely.

When the biscuits have cooled, gently melt the chocolate melts in the microwave. Spread the chocolate on the underside of the biscuits and make the squiggles with a serrated scraper or fork. Allow the chocolate to set before storing the biscuits in an airtight container. The biscuits will keep in an airtight container for 5–7 days.

Baked Spanish-style Chicken • Salmon Kebabs with Chilli & Lime • Thai-style Spiced Coriander & Almond Fish • Nut-crusted Chicken Breasts with Buttered Ginger Sauce • Steaks with Shallot & Red Wine Sauce • Butternut Pumpkin & Rocket Cannelloni with Tomato Cream Sauce • Hoisin Ginger Lamb Cutlets • Hot-Smoked Salmon Pasta with Creamy Dill & Spring Onions • Asian Chicken Burgers • Garlic Steak, Tomato & Rocket Fettuccine • Homestyle Crispy Crumbed Fish Fingers with Tartare Sauce • Sesame Fish with Green Beans & Noodles • Piña Colada Pork Cutlets • Maple-glazed Meatloaf • Chicken Cottage Pie • Honey-roasted Kumara & Ricotta Bake • Prawn & Egg Fried Rice • Red Pepper, Spinach & Pinenut Lasagne • Courgette & Baby Pea Risotto • Beef & Broccoli with Oyster Sauce • Coconut Prawn Laksa • Three-cheese Macaroni • Roast Chicken Breasts with Tomato, Pesto & Mozzarella • Simple Creamy Butter Chicken • Thai Pork & Noodles

Baked Spanish-style Chicken

Serves 4

2	chorizo sausages, sliced
2 tablespoons	olive oil
8	chicken pieces — legs, thighs, etc
1	red pepper, deseeded and chunky chopped
1	yellow pepper, deseeded and chunky chopped
3	red onions, peeled and quartered
8	cloves garlic, peeled and cut in half
400 g	can crushed tomatoes
1 cup	chicken stock
handful	rocket leaves
¼ cup	chopped pitted green or black olives

Preheat the oven to 200°C.

Fry the sliced chorizo in a large non-stick ovenproof frypan or roasting dish over a medium heat until browned. Remove from the pan and set aside.

Add the oil and chicken pieces and brown over a medium heat, turning to evenly colour. Return the chorizo to the pan with the red and yellow peppers, onions, garlic, tomatoes and stock, and bring to the boil. Place the pan in the oven and bake for 35–40 minutes until the chicken is cooked.

Sprinkle with the rocket leaves and olives.

Serve with rice, pasta or mashed potato.

Salmon Kebabs
with Chilli & Lime

Serves 4

6 tablespoons	sweet chilli sauce
	grated rind and juice of 3 limes
4 x 160 g	salmon fillets, cut into cubes
	fresh coriander leaves to garnish

Preheat the oven grill. Line a small roasting tray or oven dish with tinfoil and spray with oil.

Mix the chilli sauce, and lime rind and juice in a bowl, then divide between 2 small bowls. Thread the salmon pieces on to small metal skewers. If you are using wooden or bamboo skewers, first soak them in water for 15–20 minutes to prevent them burning under the grill.

Brush the kebabs with the chilli-lime mixture from one of the bowls to completely coat the salmon. Grill for 3–4 minutes each side.

Pour the remaining chilli-lime mixture over the kebabs just before serving.

Garnish with coriander and serve on a bed of rice with a crisp green salad on the side.

If serving larger numbers, place the fish
in little piles in a roasting dish. Blast for
8-10 minutes in a hot oven, preheated to 200°C.
Then pour the warmed sauce over the top.

Thai-style Spiced Coriander & Almond Fish

The sauce can be prepared ahead of time and reheated just before serving, making this an ideal recipe for entertaining.

Serves 6

1 kg	fresh white firm fish fillets, (about 160 g per person), chopped into chunky 5–6 cm pieces
2 tablespoons	oil
1 cup	chopped shallots or 1 large onion, peeled and roughly chopped
5	spring onions, roughly sliced
5–6 cm piece	fresh ginger, peeled
2–3 cloves	garlic, peeled
2	long red chillies, deseeded, or 1 tablespoon mild chilli paste
2 large handfuls	fresh coriander
1 cup	blanched slivered almonds
2 teaspoons	sesame oil
2 teaspoons	fish sauce
2 teaspoons	ground turmeric
2 cans	(around 800 ml) coconut milk
1 large	red pepper, deseeded and finely sliced
	salt and freshly ground black pepper
	grated rind and juice of 2–3 limes
	extra coriander to garnish

Rinse the fish pieces, cover and set aside in the fridge.

Heat the oil in a large frypan and cook the shallots or onion and the spring onions for a few minutes over a medium heat until softened. Don't let the vegetables colour or brown.

Place the ginger, garlic, chillies, coriander, almonds, sesame oil, fish sauce and turmeric in a food processor and pulse or run the machine in bursts to process the mixture to a coarse paste.

Transfer the paste to the frypan with the onion mixture. Stir in the coconut milk and red pepper, then simmer gently for around 5 minutes to allow the flavours to develop. Season with salt and pepper. Add the fish pieces and cook for 5–6 minutes. Be careful not to stir the mixture too much as you don't want the fish to break up.

Add the lime rind and juice to the sauce just before serving.

Serve with rice or noodles, and garnish with a few coriander leaves.

Variations — instead of white fish, you can use salmon, allowing 10–12 minutes to cook. The sauce can also be thinned down with fish stock, water or extra coconut milk.

Chicken fillets or boneless breasts can easily be substituted for the fish in this recipe. Allow 20–25 minutes to cook the chicken, checking it is cooked through. You can also make a great vegetarian dish with cubes of kumara, courgette and pumpkin substituted for the fish — but remember to leave the fish sauce out of the paste.

'Anyone who's interested in cooking is
interested in knowing more'

Have a confident hand
with the salt and pepper

Nut-crusted

Chicken Breasts with Buttered Ginger Sauce

Serves 4

For the sauce

½ cup	white wine
½ cup	white wine vinegar
½ cup	finely chopped shallots or onion
8	whole peppercorns
2	bay leaves
	small-egg-sized piece fresh ginger, unpeeled and roughly chopped
½ cup	cream
100 g	cold butter, cut into thumbnail-sized pieces
1 tablespoon	chopped parsley

For the chicken

4	skinless, boneless chicken breasts
2	eggs
½ cup	unsweetened natural yoghurt
1 cup	chopped fresh nuts — pecans, walnuts, macadamias, almonds, etc
1 cup	panko (Japanese) breadcrumbs
½ teaspoon	salt
	freshly ground black pepper
½ cup	oil (rice bran or canola)

Place the wine, vinegar, shallots or onion, peppercorns, bay leaves and ginger in a small saucepan over a medium-high heat. Bring to the boil and simmer for 5 minutes. Then add the cream and just bring it back to the boil. Pour through a sieve into another small saucepan and set aside. Discard the contents of the sieve.

Place a chicken breast between 2 sheets of plastic wrap. Pound the chicken into a flat schnitzel about 1.5 cm thick with the flat side of a meat mallet. Repeat with the remaining breasts.

Whisk the eggs with the yoghurt and place in a shallow dish. Place

(continued overleaf)

the chopped nuts and panko crumbs in another shallow dish and toss to combine well, then season with salt and pepper. Dip the flattened breasts into the egg mixture, then into the nut mixture, pressing down firmly so the nuts stick really well to the chicken.

Heat the oil in a large frypan and cook the breasts over a medium heat until golden brown on both sides (5 minutes each side), checking they are cooked through. Don't have the pan too hot or the crumbs will burn before the chicken has cooked properly. Drain on paper towels.

Just before serving, warm the sauce and whisk in the butter cubes until melted and the sauce is smooth and glossy. Add the chopped parsley and pour over the chicken or serve in a bowl on the side.

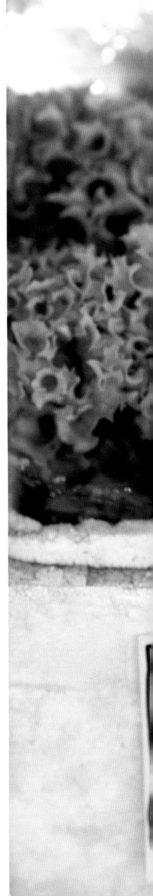

LeTTUCe
$1-80 each

Steaks with
Shallot & Red Wine Sauce

Serves 4

4	rib-eye or Scotch fillet steaks
1 cup	sliced shallots
4 tablespoons	olive oil
1 clove	garlic, crushed
	salt and freshly ground black pepper
5 tablespoons	balsamic vinegar
2 cups (500 ml)	red wine
2 cups (500 ml)	beef stock
25 g	butter, chopped into pea-sized pieces

Heat a barbecue hot plate or large frypan to medium-high and cook the steaks to medium-rare: 3–4 minutes each side, depending on the thickness of the meat. Transfer to a plate and cover with a sheet of tinfoil. Rest and keep warm while you prepare the sauce.

Place the shallots and oil in a medium-sized saucepan over a high heat and sauté for 3–4 minutes. Add the garlic and cook for another minute. Season with salt and pepper. Pour in the balsamic vinegar, red wine and stock. Bring to the boil, then turn down the heat and simmer until the mixture has reduced to about a cup. Check the seasoning, then whisk in the butter and any juices from the resting steaks.

Serve the sauce spooned over the steaks.

Butternut Pumpkin
& Rocket Cannelloni with Tomato Cream Sauce

Serves 4

400 g packet	dried lasagne sheets
2 cups	cooked, well-drained and mashed butternut pumpkin
1 bag (about 100 g)	rocket leaves, washed
1 (about 100 g)	large handful grated tasty cheese
	salt and freshly ground black pepper
2 x 400 g cans	crushed tomatoes
300 ml	cream
1 clove	garlic, crushed
2 tablespoons	chopped parsley to garnish

Preheat the oven to 180°C. Coat a small lasagne or roasting dish with non-stick baking spray.

Place 4 lasagne sheets in a large bowl. Cover with boiling water and leave to soak and soften for 5 minutes. Drain the sheets in a colander.

Place 1 lasagne sheet flat on the bench and spoon ½ cup mashed pumpkin on top, then a quarter of the rocket and a sprinkling of grated cheese. Season with salt and pepper and roll the sheet up into a log. Cut it in half if required and place in the prepared dish. Repeat with the remaining sheets, pumpkin, rocket and cheese, reserving some cheese for the top.

Mix the tomatoes, cream and garlic together in a bowl, and season with salt and pepper. Pour the sauce over the rolled cannelloni and sprinkle with grated cheese.

Bake for 15–20 minutes until heated through and bubbling. Scatter the chopped parsley over and serve with a green salad.

Easy entertaining may seem like
a contradiction in terms.

Makes both the cook
and the guests happy.

Hoisin Ginger
Lamb Cutlets

Serves 4

12–16	trimmed lamb cutlets (3–4 per person)
1 cup	hoisin sauce
2 tablespoons	soy sauce
2 tablespoons	lemon juice
3 cm piece	ginger, peeled and grated

Place the cutlets in a large zip-lock plastic bag with the hoisin and soy sauces, lemon juice and ginger. Close the bag and squish to completely coat the cutlets in the marinade.

Place the bag in the fridge for at least 2 hours, or overnight to use the following day.

Spray a large frypan with oil and heat to medium-high. Pat the cutlets dry with paper towels, reserving the bag of marinade, then place in the pan and cook for about 5 minutes each side, until browned and medium rare. Remove from the pan and rest, keeping warm.

Squeeze out all the marinade from the plastic bag into the pan and heat until the sauce is bubbling.

Arrange the cutlets on plates, pour the sauce over them and serve with a side of green vegetables and mashed potatoes.

Hot-Smoked Salmon
Pasta with Creamy Dill & Spring Onions

Serves 4

400 g	dried fusilli or similar pasta
5	spring onions, thinly sliced
3 tablespoons	chopped fresh dill, or 3 teaspoons dried dill tips
¼ cup	toasted pinenuts
1 cup	cream or reduced-fat evaporated milk
200 g	hot-smoked skinless, boneless salmon fillet, flaked into small pieces
	salt and freshly ground black pepper
	grated rind and juice of 2 lemons

Warm 4 serving bowls.

Bring a large saucepan of salted water to the boil. Cook the pasta according to the packet instructions. Drain, reserving 1 cup of the pasta water.

Place the saucepan back on the heat, add the spring onions, dill, pinenuts, cream and flaked salmon and warm through. Season with salt and pepper, and add the lemon rind and juice. Add the cooked pasta and stir to coat with the sauce. If the sauce is a little dry, thin it down with some of the reserved pasta water.

Serve immediately in the warmed bowls.

Asian
Chicken Burgers

Makes 4

2	skinless, boneless chicken breasts, chopped into bite-sized pieces
2 tablespoons	hoisin sauce
2 tablespoons	sweet chilli sauce
1 clove	garlic, crushed
1 handful	fresh coriander leaves and stalks
	salt and freshly ground black pepper
1 tablespoon	oil
4	hamburger buns
4 tablespoons	mayonnaise
4	lettuce leaves
2	tomatoes, sliced
1	cucumber, peeled lengthwise into ribbons
1 small bunch	snowpea shoots
	sweet chilli sauce to serve

Place the chicken pieces, hoisin and sweet chilli sauces, garlic, coriander, salt and pepper in a food processor, and process until the mixture is thoroughly combined and looks like mince. Mould into 4 patties.

Heat the oil in a large non-stick frypan and cook the patties over a medium-high heat until golden brown on both sides and cooked through (about 2 minutes on each side).

Cut the buns in half and toast. Spread the bottom halves with mayonnaise and layer on the lettuce, tomato, cucumber and snowpea shoots. Top with a pattie and drizzle with a little sweet chilli sauce. Top with the other half of each bun.

Using disposable gloves makes shaping the patties a much less messy job.

Garlic Steak,
Tomato & Rocket Fettuccine

Serves 4

350 g	dried fettuccine
2 tablespoons	olive oil
1	onion, finely chopped
2 cloves	garlic, crushed
2 teaspoons	tomato purée
½ cup	red wine or beef stock
400 g can	crushed tomatoes
	salt and freshly ground black pepper
500 g	sirloin steak
1 cup	cherry tomatoes
2 handfuls	baby rocket leaves
	extra-virgin olive oil for drizzling

Bring a large saucepan of salted water to the boil and cook the fettuccine according to the packet instructions.

While the pasta is cooking, heat the oil in a frypan and gently fry the onion and garlic over a medium heat for 5 minutes. Then add the tomato purée, red wine or stock, and canned tomatoes. Bring to the boil, then lower the heat and simmer for 8–10 minutes to reduce the liquid. Season with salt and pepper.

In a medium-sized non-stick frypan, cook the steak over a high heat for 2 timed minutes on each side. Remove to a plate, cover with tinfoil and rest for 5 minutes before slicing.

Drain the pasta and toss with the sauce and sliced steak. Scatter the cherry tomatoes and rocket leaves over.

Divide between 4 serving plates, drizzle with a splash of extra-virgin olive oil and add an extra grind of pepper.

Resting allows the juices of the steak to be
reabsorbed and the meat will be tender, pink and
not bloody when you slice it.

Homestyle

Crispy Crumbed Fish Fingers with Tartare Sauce

Serves 4

2	eggs, beaten
2 cups	panko (Japanese) breadcrumbs
	grated rind of 1 medium-sized lemon
½ teaspoon	salt
	freshly ground black pepper
500 g	skinned and boned firm white fish fillets — cod, snapper or tarakihi — sliced into Weet-Bix-sized strips

For the tartare sauce

2 tablespoons	capers, finely chopped
2 tablespoons	chopped parsley
1 tablespoon	chopped chives
1 teaspoon	lemon-pepper seasoning
1 cup	prepared thick creamy mayonnaise
1 tablespoon	wholegrain mustard
	juice of 1 medium-sized lemon (use the one you've grated the rind of)

Preheat the oven to 200°C. Coat an oven tray with spray oil.

Pour the eggs into a shallow dish. Mix the panko crumbs, lemon rind, salt and pepper together and tip into another shallow dish. Dip the fish strips in the egg, then in the crumbs, pressing down so they stick well to the fish. Place on the oven tray, leaving a little room between each.

Bake for 15 minutes, then carefully turn over to brown the underside, cooking for a further 5–6 minutes.

Mix the sauce ingredients together in a bowl.

Divide the fish fingers between 4 plates and serve the sauce in a dish on the side. A green vegetable or salad is the perfect accompaniment.

Sesame Fish
with Green Beans & Noodles

Serves 4

600–700 g	fresh skinned and boned fish fillets — cod, snapper, salmon, etc — cut into chunky bite-sized pieces
6 tablespoons	sweet chilli sauce
2 tablespoons	fish sauce
1 tablespoon	sesame oil
2 tablespoons	rice wine or sushi vinegar
2 tablespoons	oil (rice bran or canola)
5	spring onions, sliced diagonally
1 handful (100 g)	green beans, chopped into short lengths
2 bunches	pak choi, sliced
3 handfuls (250 g)	thin dried rice noodles
1 tablespoon	toasted sesame seeds
1 tablespoon	black sesame seeds (optional)
2	limes, cut into wedges to serve

Place the chunks of fish in a bowl with the sweet chilli and fish sauces, sesame oil and vinegar. Stir to coat the fish well. Marinate for 10 minutes.

Heat the oil in a large frypan over a medium heat. Place the fish pieces in the pan, reserving the marinade, and cook for just a couple of minutes. Add the spring onions, beans and pak choi, and stir-fry to heat the vegetables. Then add in the marinade mixture and heat through.

Soak the noodles in boiling water to soften, according to the packet instructions. Drain and add to the pan with the sesame seeds.

Serve with the lime wedges to squeeze over.

Piña Colada
Pork Cutlets

Serves 4

4	boneless pork cutlets
	grated rind and juice of 2 limes
1 cup	coconut cream or milk
1 cup	drained crushed pineapple
½ cup	chopped coriander
3 tablespoons	sweet chilli sauce
1	red pepper, deseeded and thinly sliced
	extra coriander leaves to garnish

Barbecue, grill or panfry the pork cutlets on a medium-high heat for about 4 minutes on each side until just nicely cooked through.

While the pork is cooking, place the lime rind and juice, coconut cream, crushed pineapple, chopped coriander, chilli sauce and some of the pepper slices, in a small saucepan over a medium-high heat. Simmer the sauce for only as long as it takes the pork to cook.

To serve, arrange the pork on plates, pour the sauce over it and garnish with the reserved pepper slices and extra coriander leaves. This is great with rice or pasta, and a green salad.

Maple-glazed Meatloaf

Serves 4–6, with leftovers

500 g	beef mince
500 g	sausage meat
2 cloves	garlic, crushed
1	onion, finely chopped
1 tablespoon	finely chopped fresh thyme
1 teaspoon	ground cumin
1 teaspoon	ground coriander
1 tablespoon	finely chopped parsley
¼ cup	barbecue sauce
2 tablespoons	Worcestershire sauce
1	egg, lightly beaten
	salt and freshly ground black pepper
¼ cup	maple syrup
¼ cup	tomato sauce

Preheat the oven to 180°C. Coat a 10 x 20 x 7 cm loaf tin with non-stick baking spray.

Place all the ingredients, except the maple syrup and tomato sauce, in a large mixing bowl. Mix well until thoroughly combined. Season with salt and pepper.

Stir the maple syrup and tomato sauce together in a bowl until blended, and set aside.

Place the meat mixture in the prepared tin and press down well. Brush with half the maple-syrup glaze.

Bake for 30 minutes, then brush with the remaining glaze. Bake a further 20–30 minutes until the loaf is cooked through. Allow to cool in the tin for 10 minutes before turning out.

Serve sliced, with mashed potatoes and a green salad or vegetables.

A pinch of panache,
a dash of nostalgia.

Chicken
Cottage Pie

Serves 4

1 tablespoon	olive oil
1 large	onion, finely chopped
500 g	skinless, boneless chicken thighs, cut in chunks
1 cup	chicken stock
1 cup	sweetcorn (frozen or canned)
½ cup	crème fraîche
3 tablespoons	coarsely chopped parsley
	salt and freshly ground black pepper
1 kg	potatoes (I use Agria), peeled and cut into chunks
2 tablespoons	butter or extra crème fraîche

Preheat the oven to 200°C.

Heat the oil in a large frypan and cook the onion and chicken over a medium-high heat for 6–8 minutes, until the onion is soft and the chicken is lightly browned. Pour in the stock and simmer gently for 15–20 minutes until the chicken is cooked through. Stir in the sweetcorn, crème fraîche and parsley, and season with salt and pepper.

In a saucepan of lightly salted water, boil the potatoes until tender. Drain and pass through a potato ricer or mash with the butter or extra crème fraîche. Season with salt and pepper.

Spoon the chicken mixture into a medium pie dish. Top with the mashed potato and bake for 20–25 minutes until golden brown.

Variation — peas or mixed vegetables can be added to the chicken mixture.

Honey-roasted
Kumara & Ricotta Bake

Serves 6–8

2 tablespoons	oil (rice bran or canola)
6	kumara, peeled and sliced
4 tablespoons	runny honey
6	eggs, beaten
3 cloves	garlic, crushed
400 g	ricotta
	salt and freshly ground black pepper
1 bunch	spinach, washed and stalks removed
2	red peppers, deseeded and chopped
¼ cup	fresh basil leaves
1 cup	grated Parmesan

Preheat the oven to 170°C. Coat a casserole or small lasagne dish with non-stick baking spray.

Place the oil and kumara slices in a roasting dish. Drizzle the honey over, turning the slices to coat both sides. Bake for 15–20 minutes until tender.

Mix the eggs, garlic and ricotta together in a bowl. Season with salt and pepper to taste.

Line the base of the prepared dish with half the roasted kumara slices. Spread all the spinach over the kumara, then sprinkle with the chopped peppers and basil leaves. Pour over half the ricotta mixture and sprinkle with ½ cup Parmesan. Top with the remaining kumara, pour the rest of the ricotta over the top and scatter with the remaining ½ cup Parmesan.

Bake for 30–40 minutes or until lightly browned and firm.

If you are a bit stressed about entertaining and find yourself angst-ing about what people will think – just relax, take a breath and think, 'What's the worst that can happen and who cares.'

Prawn & Egg
Fried Rice

Serves 4

1½ cups	basmati rice
2 tablespoons	oil (rice bran or canola)
2 cloves	garlic, crushed
1	red chilli, deseeded and finely sliced
3	eggs, lightly beaten
1 cup	frozen peas
5	spring onions, finely sliced
2 cups	cooked prawns (you can use thawed precooked frozen prawns)
1 tablespoon	soy sauce
	extra soy sauce to serve (optional)

Cook the rice in boiling salted water for about 12 minutes until just tender. Drain.

Heat the oil in a large frypan and stir-fry the garlic and chilli over a medium heat for 30 seconds, being careful not to burn them. Add the drained rice and coat well with the oil, chilli and garlic. Cook for about 1 minute.

Push the rice to the edges of the pan and pour the eggs into the cleared centre. Scramble the eggs, stirring to cook evenly.

Add the peas and spring onions, and mix the rice back in. Then add the prawns and soy sauce, and heat through.

Serve with extra soy sauce if desired.

Red Pepper, Spinach & Pinenut Lasagne

Serves 4–6

5	red peppers, deseeded and thickly sliced
2 tablespoons	olive oil
2 tablespoons	balsamic vinegar
4 cloves	garlic, crushed or finely chopped
1 packet (100 g)	baby spinach leaves
	béchamel sauce (see below)
400 g packet	fresh lasagne sheets (you will need at least 3 sheets)
3 cups	grated mozzarella
½ cup	pinenuts
For the béchamel sauce	
600 ml	milk
2	bay leaves
50 g	butter
3 tablespoons	flour
1 teaspoon	Dijon mustard
1 cup	grated or shaved Parmesan
	salt and freshly ground black pepper

Preheat the oven to 180°C. Coat a lasagne dish with non-stick baking spray.

Place the pepper slices in a roasting dish and drizzle with the olive oil and vinegar. Roast for 25 minutes, then add the garlic and roast for a further 3 minutes. The peppers will be soft, with the skins blackening.

Microwave the spinach until wilted.

To make the sauce, place the milk and bay leaves in a medium-sized saucepan over a medium-high heat. Heat until almost boiling, then reduce the heat and simmer for 3 minutes. Be careful the milk doesn't boil over. Melt the butter in a frypan over a medium heat and whisk in the flour, cooking it for about 1 minute. Remove the bay leaves from the milk and then gradually pour the milk into the frypan, whisking to ensure a nice smooth sauce. Add the mustard and half the Parmesan, and season generously with salt and pepper.

Spoon a third of the sauce into the base of the prepared lasagne dish. Top with a third of the cooked pepper mixture, wilted spinach and the mozzarella. Cover with a sheet of lasagne. Repeat the layers, finishing with a final layer of sauce. Sprinkle the remaining Parmesan and the pinenuts over the top.

Bake for 20–25 minutes.

Serve with a crisp green salad.

New foods shout their health benefits on the front label, yet bewilder us with the fine print on the back.

Courgette & Baby Pea
Risotto

Serves 4

1 tablespoon	olive oil
5	spring onions, finely chopped
2 cloves	garlic, crushed
3	tomatoes, roughly chopped
350 g	arborio rice
1½ litres	chicken or vegetable stock
3	medium courgettes, finely chopped
2 cups	baby peas (fresh or frozen)
	salt and freshly ground black pepper
handful	basil leaves, torn into little pieces
	shaved or grated Parmesan to serve (optional)

Heat the oil in a large frypan and cook the spring onions and garlic over a medium heat for 2–3 minutes. Add the chopped tomatoes and the rice. Pour in 2 cups of the stock, stirring while it comes to the boil and the liquid starts to be absorbed. Pour in the rest of the stock and stir a couple of times during the next 5–6 minutes. Then add the courgettes and peas, and stir until the liquid is completely absorbed and the rice tender. The mixture should be a thick soupy consistency and not too dry. Season with salt and pepper, and scatter the basil leaves on top.

Serve immediately with the Parmesan on top, if using.

Beef & Broccoli
with Oyster Sauce

Serves 4

2 tablespoons	oil (rice bran or canola)
4	rump steaks, trimmed of all fat and sliced into strips
5	spring onions, sliced
2 tablespoons	finely chopped or grated fresh ginger
2 cloves	garlic, crushed
1 large head	broccoli, broken into florets and blanched for 2 minutes
½ cup	oyster sauce
¼ cup	water
1	red chilli, deseeded and finely sliced, to garnish

Heat the oil in a large non-stick frypan or wok over a high heat and quickly brown the strips of meat. Remove from the pan and set aside. Add the spring onions, reserving a few slices for garnishing, the ginger and garlic, and stir-fry for 2 minutes.

Return the beef strips along with the blanched broccoli to the pan or wok. Stir in the oyster sauce. Rinse the ½ cup measure with ¼ cup water, and add this to the pan. Stir-fry for 3–4 minutes, until the mixture is heated through.

Serve on rice with the reserved spring onion and sliced chilli to garnish.

Coconut
Prawn Laksa

Serves 4

2 tablespoons	oil (rice bran or canola)
2 cloves	garlic, crushed
4	spring onions, finely chopped
2 tablespoons	finely chopped or grated fresh ginger
2	long green or red chillies, deseeded and finely chopped
3 tablespoons	chopped coriander
	grated rind and juice of 2 limes
400 g	raw prawns
400 ml can	coconut milk
500 ml	chicken stock
1 packet (150 g)	egg noodles
	salt and freshly ground black pepper
	coriander leaves to garnish

Heat the oil in a large frypan and cook the garlic, spring onions, ginger and chillies over a medium-high heat for 2–3 minutes. Then add the coriander and lime rind and juice, and give the mixture a quick stir.

Add the prawns, coconut milk and stock and simmer for 5 minutes to cook the prawns and allow the flavours to develop. Add the noodles and simmer for a further 3–4 minutes until the noodles have softened. Season with salt and pepper to taste.

Serve in noodle bowls with coriander leaves for garnish.

Three-cheese
Macaroni

Serves 4

50 g	butter
4 tablespoons	flour
1 litre	milk
1 clove	garlic, crushed
1 teaspoon	Dijon mustard
	salt and freshly ground black pepper
2 large handfuls (around 200 g)	grated tasty cheese
1 large handful (around 100 g)	grated gruyère or edam
½ cup	grated Parmesan
300 g	dried macaroni

Preheat the oven to 200°C. Coat 4 small ovenproof dishes with non-stick baking spray.

Melt the butter in a small saucepan over a medium heat and whisk in the flour. Cook gently for about a minute. Then gradually whisk in the milk to make a smooth sauce. Add the garlic and mustard, and season to taste with salt and lots of pepper. Stir in the tasty and gruyère cheeses and half the Parmesan, until melted.

Bring a saucepan of salted water to the boil and cook the macaroni according to the packet instructions. Drain and rinse in cold water.

Add the drained macaroni to the sauce, mix well, then divide between the prepared dishes. Sprinkle with the remaining Parmesan.

Bake for 15–20 minutes until golden and bubbling.

Imagination not elaboration is the
key to a sparkling dinner party.

Some people know just how to throw a party. They have a special talent for making any event relaxed and memorable!

Roast Chicken Breasts
with Tomato, Pesto & Mozzarella

Serves 4

6	green olives, pitted and chopped
1 small clove	garlic, crushed
2 teaspoons	basil pesto
250 g	cream cheese (not softened or light)
1 cup	grated mozzarella
4	skinless, boneless chicken breasts
	salt and freshly ground black pepper
4	tomatoes, thinly sliced
2 tablespoons	olive oil

Preheat the oven to 220°C.

Mix the chopped olives, crushed garlic, pesto, cream cheese and mozzarella together in a bowl until well combined.

Cut a pocket in the side of each chicken breast. Stuff the cream cheese mixture into the pockets, pressing down firmly to close each pocket. Season with salt and pepper. Place the chicken breasts in a roasting dish and lay the tomato slices on top. Drizzle with olive oil and an extra grind of pepper.

Roast for 20–25 minutes until the chicken breasts are cooked through and the tomato is roasted and a little shrivelled looking.

Serve with a crisp green salad.

The mozzarella mixed with the cream cheese helps the filling stay together and not ooze out of the chicken breasts.

Simple Creamy
Butter Chicken

Serves 4

2 tablespoons	oil (rice bran or canola)
4	skinless, boneless chicken breasts, cut into bite-sized pieces
1 large	onion, chopped
2 cloves	garlic, crushed
1 tablespoon	grated fresh ginger
1 teaspoon	ground turmeric
1 teaspoon	ground cumin
2 teaspoons	garam masala
1 teaspoon	mild chilli paste
400 g can	crushed tomatoes
375 ml can	evaporated milk (you can use low fat)
1 bunch	coriander, chopped
½ cup	thick natural yoghurt
	poppadoms to serve
	coriander leaves to garnish

Heat the oil in a large frypan and cook the chicken over a medium-high heat for 3–4 minutes until browned. Remove from the pan and set aside. Add the onion, garlic and ginger to the pan and stir-fry for 3–4 minutes until the onion has softened. Add the turmeric, cumin, garam masala and chilli paste, and cook for a further minute. Add the tomatoes with their juice and simmer for 5 minutes, letting the mixture thicken and the flavours develop. Return the chicken to the pan with the evaporated milk. Stir through the coriander and bring to the boil.

Serve with basmati rice, a dollop of yoghurt and poppadoms on the side. Garnish with a few coriander leaves.

Thai
Pork & Noodles

Serves 4

2 tablespoons	olive oil
500 g	pork sausage meat (you can squeeze the meat out of 4–5 sausages)
1 teaspoon	finely chopped lemongrass (white part only)
½	red chilli, deseeded and finely chopped
1	red onion, chopped
2 cloves	garlic, crushed
200 g packet	soft noodles — Hokkien or Singapore
3 tablespoons	fish sauce
	grated rind and juice of 2 limes
2 tablespoons	sweet chilli sauce
1 handful	fresh mint leaves

Heat the oil in a large frypan or wok on high. Drop bite-sized pieces of the sausage meat into the oil and fry until golden brown.

Add the lemongrass, chilli, red onion and garlic and stir-fry for a minute before adding the noodles, breaking up the bundle as they go in the pan. Then add the fish sauce, lime rind and juice, and sweet chilli sauce. Fry for a couple of minutes to heat the mixture through.

Add the mint leaves just before serving.

Strawberry Citrus Cheesecake • Peach Puddycake • Mars Bar Ice-cream • Over-the-top Butterscotch Sauce • Crème Brûlée • Microwave Sticky Chocolate Mud Pudding • Banoffee Creams • Powder-puff Chocolate Mousse • St Clement's Puddings • Raspberry Jam & Whipped Cream Roulade • Lemon Meringue

Rolled Pavlova • Thick Lemon Curd • Feijoa Butterscotch Self-saucing Sticky Puds • Creamy Coconut & Lemon Custard Cake • Fresh Fruit Salad with Citrus Syrup • Fruit Marshmallow Kebabs • Rhubarb Berry Oat Crumble • Roast Figs with Blue Cheese • Raspberry Mousse • Piped Meringues

Strawberry Citrus Cheesecake

Serves 6–8

1 x 250 g packet	plain wine, digestive or gingernut biscuits
125 g	butter, melted
1 x 85 g packet	strawberry jelly crystals
¾ cup	boiling water
	grated rind and juice of 1 lemon
	grated rind of 1 orange
1 punnet (about 2 cups)	strawberries, stalks removed
400 g	cream cheese (not light or softened)
¾ cup	caster sugar
375 ml can	evaporated milk, well chilled

Coat a 21 cm springform tin with non-stick baking spray and line the base with non-stick baking paper.

Place the biscuits in a food processor and process into crumbs. Then add the melted butter and process until combined. Press into the base of the prepared tin. Refrigerate for about 1 hour until firm.

Dissolve the jelly crystals in the boiling water. Add the lemon rind and juice and the orange rind, and mix well. Mash the strawberries with a fork until puréed, reserving a few whole ones for decoration, then add to the jelly mixture.

Beat the cream cheese and sugar together until smooth and creamy. Stir in the jelly, mixing until well combined and smooth.

Beat the chilled milk with an electric mixer until very thick, then gently fold into the jelly and cream cheese mixture. Pour over the base and refrigerate for at least 4 hours until set firm.

Carefully unclip and remove the side of the tin, then slide the cheesecake off the paper-lined base on to a serving plate. Serve decorated with the reserved strawberries.

Peach
Puddycake

Serves 6

2 cups	flour
1 cup	icing sugar
250 g	cold butter, cubed
8	peach halves (fresh or canned; peeled if fresh)
1 teaspoon	ground cinnamon
1 tablespoon	caster sugar
2	egg yolks
250 ml	cream
2 tablespoons	extra caster sugar
	icing sugar to dust

Coat a 20 cm round springform cake tin with non-stick baking spray and line the base with non-stick baking paper.

Place the flour, icing sugar and cold butter in a food processor and process until the mixture clumps around the blade. Press the pastry into the base and up the sides of the prepared tin. Chill in the freezer for 30 minutes. Meanwhile, preheat the oven to 180°C.

Drain the peaches if using canned ones. Remove the pastry-lined tin from the freezer and place the peach halves cut side down on the base. Sprinkle with the cinnamon and tablespoon of caster sugar.

Bake for 20 minutes.

With the oven still on, beat the egg yolks, cream and extra caster sugar together and pour over the baked peach halves.

Return the cake to the oven and bake for a further 30–35 minutes until the custard is just set. Cool for 10–15 minutes in the tin, then carefully unclip and remove the side of the tin and slide the cake off the base on to a serving plate. Dust with icing sugar and serve with softly whipped cream or ice-cream.

Sweet

Some people insist that no meal is complete without a sweet finale. Actually some people I know would prefer to skip the main entirely and go straight to dessert.

These are worth saving room for.

Prepared custard is available in the dairy section of supermarkets and is a cheat's way of using a custard base for ice-cream.

Mars Bar
Ice-cream

Serves 4

3 x 53 g	Mars Bars
1 cup	cream
2 cups	prepared custard

Chop up one of the Mars Bars into small pieces. Melt the other 2 in the cream, either in a small saucepan over a medium heat or in the microwave, stirring until well combined and smooth. Mix in the custard and chopped Mars Bar. Pour into a small plastic container and freeze.

Remove from the freezer 5–10 minutes before serving so the ice-cream is easier to scoop.

Over-the-top
Butterscotch Sauce

This is a totally decadent, rich and serious butterscotch sauce — only to be used for very special occasions. It is delicious poured over ice-cream.

Makes 3 cups

400 g can	sweetened condensed milk
50 g	butter
300 ml	cream
2 cups	brown sugar

Place all the ingredients in a saucepan and stir over a medium heat until the butter melts, and the mixture combines and comes to the boil. Keep stirring while the sauce comes to boiling point as it can burn easily.

Cool and then pour into a squeezy bottle. Keeps in the fridge for 2–3 weeks.

'Guardian angels up above keep-
an eye on those I love.'

Crème
Brûlée

Makes 6

2 cups (500 ml)	cream
1 teaspoon	vanilla bean paste
4	egg yolks
¼ cup	caster sugar
For the caramel	
½ cup	sugar
1 tablespoon	water

Preheat the oven to 160°C.

Place the cream and vanilla paste in a small saucepan over a low heat and heat gently until it just comes to the boil. Remove from the heat and allow to cool slightly.

Beat the egg yolks and caster sugar together until thick and pale. Pour in the cream while continuing to whisk until well combined. Return the mixture to the saucepan and stir over a very gentle heat until the creamy custard has thickened and coats the back of a spoon.

Pour the custard into 6 x ¾ cup-capacity ovenproof ramekins or small dishes. Place the ramekins in a deep-sided baking dish and pour hot water into the dish to come three-quarters of the way up the sides of the ramekins. I find it easier to place the dish in the oven with the oven tray pulled slightly out and to pour the water from an electric jug.

Bake for 25–30 minutes until the custard is just firm and set. Remove from the oven and refrigerate for 5–6 hours until really chilled.

To make the caramel, place the sugar and 1 tablespoon of water in a saucepan and bring to the boil. Continue to boil, without stirring to achieve a pale caramel colour. Remove from the heat and place the saucepan base in cold water — this stops the caramel from colouring too much. Carefully pour on top of each crème brûlée and allow to set.

Microwave Sticky
Chocolate Mud Pudding

Serves 4–6

100 g	butter, melted
1 cup	self-raising flour
3 tablespoons	dark baking cocoa
¾ cup	sugar
½ cup	milk
1 teaspoon	vanilla
For the sauce	
¾ cup	brown sugar
2 tablespoons	dark baking cocoa
1½ cups	boiling water

Coat a 23 cm microwave-proof ring mould with non-stick baking spray.

Mix the melted butter, flour, cocoa, sugar, milk and vanilla together in a medium-sized bowl of an electric mixer until well combined. Pour into the prepared mould.

To make the sauce, mix the brown sugar and cocoa together in a bowl and sprinkle over the top of the chocolate pudding. Pour the boiling water over the top.

Microwave on high for 6 minutes. Then leave to rest and cool for another 6 minutes.

Serve with whipped cream or ice-cream.

This recipe was tested in a 1000-watt microwave. Higher or lower powered microwaves may require a slight variation in timing.

Banoffee Creams

Makes 6 large or 9 small — but incredibly rich — desserts

½ packet (125 g)	gingernut biscuits
40 g (200 g)	butter, melted
½ can	caramel sweetened condensed milk
1	banana
300 ml	cream
1 teaspoon	vanilla
2 tablespoons	icing sugar
1 teaspoon	powdered gelatine
2 tablespoons	hot strong coffee
1	Flake bar, crumbled

Coat individual loose-bottomed moulds with non-stick baking spray.

Place the gingernuts in a food processor and process into crumbs. Then add the melted butter and process until well combined. Divide the base mixture between the prepared moulds and press down firmly. Refrigerate for 30 minutes.

Remove from the fridge and pour the condensed milk over the bases, smoothing the tops level. Slice the banana and place the slices on top of the condensed milk.

Whip the cream with the vanilla and icing sugar. Add the gelatine to the hot coffee, stirring until it dissolves. Fold the coffee mixture into the whipped cream. Spoon the whipped cream over the banana so the moulds are full.

Place in the refrigerator for 3–4 hours until firm and set. Carefully press out the bottom of each mould. Sprinkle the tops of the creams with the crumbled Flake.

Powder-puff
Chocolate Mousse

Makes 10–12 shot glasses

3 teaspoons (10 g packet)	powdered gelatine
3 tablespoons	cold water
200 ml	cream
250 g	dark chocolate (more than 40% cocoa solids), chopped
500 ml	cream, softly whipped
	extra whipped cream to decorate (optional)
	chopped or shaved chocolate to decorate (optional)

Place the gelatine in a small bowl or cup and stir in the cold water. The gelatine will soak up the water and the granules will soften.

Pour the first measure of cream into a small saucepan and stir over a medium heat, just bringing it to the boil. Remove from the heat as soon as the cream boils and stir in the spongy, soaked gelatine until it has dissolved. Then add the chocolate, stirring until it has all melted.

Cool but don't refrigerate the mixture or it will set firm. When it is at room temperature, fold the chocolate mixture into the softly whipped cream until smoothly combined.

Pour or, using a piping bag with a star nozzle, pipe into small shot glasses, espresso cups or tiny bowls. Decorate the mousse with extra whipped cream and chopped or shaved chocolate, if using.

St Clement's
Puddings

Makes 6 little 1-cup puddings

50 g	butter
1 cup	caster sugar
½ cup	flour
	grated rind and juice of 1 small lemon
	grated rind and juice of ½ orange
	grated rind and juice of 2 small limes
3	eggs, separated
275 ml	milk
	icing sugar to dust

Preheat the oven to 180°C. Coat 6 x 1-cup-capacity ovenproof pudding dishes with non-stick baking spray.

Beat the butter and caster sugar together. Add the flour and grated rinds and juices, and mix together well. Then mix in the egg yolks and milk.

Beat the egg whites until stiff and carefully fold into the pudding mixture. Spoon into the prepared dishes.

Bake for 14–16 minutes until puffed and golden.

Dust with icing sugar and serve with ice-cream or softly whipped cream.

Raspberry Jam & Whipped Cream Roulade

Serves 8–10

4	eggs, at room temperature
½ cup	caster sugar
½ cup	self-raising flour
300 ml	cream
½ cup	raspberry jam
	icing sugar to dust

Preheat the oven to 200°C. Line a large 25 x 35 cm large sponge-roll tin with non-stick baking paper and coat the paper with non-stick baking spray. Trim the paper so it is level with the sides of the tin, making sure there isn't any overhang.

Beat the eggs and caster sugar together with an electric mixer until pale and creamy. Sift the flour and fold it into the egg mixture. Spread in the prepared tin. Bake for 7–8 minutes until a pale-golden toast colour and the cake is pulling away from the sides of the tin.

Turn out on to a fresh sheet of baking paper and cool completely. Lightly score a line with a serrated knife, 2 cm from one of the long edges of the cake — this will help with the rolling.

Whip the cream until thick. Spread the raspberry jam evenly over the cooled cake and cover with whipped cream. You may not need to use all the cream. Using the baking paper, roll the roulade towards you, starting with the scored-edge side. Keep the roll tight and round like a sushi roll.

Dust with icing sugar and serve with extra whipped cream if desired, or freeze until needed.

Variation — this versatile roulade can be filled with fruit yoghurt, lemon curd, any flavour of jam, or sliced fruit and cream. To make an Arctic Roll, fill with softened ice-cream, roll up and freeze.

Lemon Meringue
Rolled Pavlova

Serves 6–8

6	egg whites
2 cups	caster sugar
1 teaspoon	cornflour
1 teaspoon	vanilla
1 teaspoon	malt vinegar
½ cup	flaked almonds
	icing sugar to dust
300 ml	cream, whipped
1 cup	lemon curd (see recipe on page 266)

Preheat the oven to 150°C. Coat a 25 x 35 cm sponge-roll or slice tin with non-stick baking spray and line with non-stick baking paper.

Beat the egg whites in a large metal, china or glass bowl (not plastic) with an electric mixer until really foamy. Slowly, with the mixer still going, add the caster sugar, a spoonful at a time until all the sugar has been incorporated and the meringue is thick and glossy white. Fold in the cornflour, vanilla and vinegar.

Spoon into the prepared tin, spreading to the edges, and sprinkle with the flaked almond.

Bake for 25 minutes.

Lay a sheet of baking paper on a flat surface and sprinkle with icing sugar. Turn the pavlova out on the baking paper, almond side down. Cool completely.

When cold, spread with the whipped cream and dollop the lemon curd on top. Using the baking paper to help you, roll up from the long side into a round log shape. Don't worry if the surface cracks. Transfer carefully to a serving platter or board, and dust again with icing sugar before slicing to serve.

Thick Lemon Curd

Makes 3 cups

200 g	butter
1 cup	caster sugar
	grated rind and juice of 3 lemons
4	eggs

Melt the butter in a saucepan over a medium-high heat. Whisk the sugar, lemon rind and juice and eggs into the butter until well combined. Whisk continuously while the curd thickens and comes to the boil. Remove from the heat just as it is about to boil vigorously, and cool.

When cold, store the curd covered in the fridge. It will thicken considerably in the fridge and will keep for 2–3 weeks.

Variations   – after making the curd, add ½ cup passionfruit pulp or squashed raspberries or banana.

There is no way you can be a perfect host at a dinner party, but millions of ways to be a good one.

Feijoa Butterscotch
Self-saucing Sticky Puds

Makes 6

¾ cup	brown sugar
1 cup	self-raising flour
¼ cup	milk
1	egg
1 teaspoon	vanilla
100 g	butter, melted
3 tablespoons	golden syrup
6 large	feijoas, halved
6 tablespoons	extra brown sugar
1½ cups	boiling water
	icing sugar to dust

Preheat the oven to 180°C. Coat 6 x 1-cup-capacity ovenproof ramekins or small pudding bowls with non-stick baking spray.

Place the first measure of brown sugar, the flour, milk, egg, vanilla and melted butter in a food processor and mix until smooth, scraping down the sides of the bowl so the mixture is thoroughly combined.

Pour equal amounts of the golden syrup into the bottom of each ramekin. Scoop out the feijoa pulp, keeping it intact, and slice into each ramekin. Pour the batter over the top of the feijoas, filling each ramekin to just three-quarters full. Sprinkle each pudding with a tablespoon of extra brown sugar, then gently pour ¼ cup of boiling water into each ramekin. Do not mix the water in, just carefully pour it on top.

Bake for 20–25 minutes, until the puddings have risen and are firm, set and golden brown.

Serve immediately with a dusting of icing sugar and, if desired, a scoop of vanilla ice-cream.

Creamy Coconut &
(Lemon Custard Cake

A totally simple recipe that always gets raves and requests for second servings.

Serves 6

4	eggs
½ cup	flour
1 cup	brown sugar, firmly packed
1 cup	fine desiccated coconut
125 g	butter, melted
300 ml	cream
¾ cup	milk
	grated rind of 2 lemons
¼ cup	lemon juice
	icing sugar to dust
	fresh fruit to serve

Preheat the oven to 180°C. Coat a 20 cm cake tin with non-stick baking spray and line the sides and base with non-stick baking paper.

Place all the ingredients, except the icing sugar and fresh fruit, into a food processor or blender and process to a smooth batter. Pour into the prepared tin.

Bake for 40–45 minutes until browned and fully set in the centre.

If serving warm, allow the cake to rest for 20–25 minutes before cutting. Dust with icing sugar, cut into portions and serve with fruit. This cake is just as delicious cold.

Fresh Fruit Salad

with Citrus Syrup

Serves 4–6

For the syrup

½ cup	sugar
1¼ cups	water
	grated rind and juice of 1 lemon
	grated rind and juice of 1 orange
	grated rind and juice of 1 lime

For the fruit salad

1	orange, peeled and cut into pieces
1	apple, peeled and cut into thick slices
1	kiwifruit, peeled and cut into cubes
¼	rock melon, peeled and cut into cubes
1 slice	fresh pineapple, cut into cubes
¼	small watermelon, peeled and cut into cubes
10	grapes, cut in half lengthwise and deseeded
1	peach or nectarine, pitted and sliced
	strawberries or other available fresh fruit

Place all the syrup ingredients in a saucepan over a medium heat and bring to the boil. Strain into a jug, then chill.

Toss the fruit together in a bowl. Pour the chilled syrup over and mix gently to combine.

Any seasonal fresh fruit can be used in the fruit salad. If desired, scoop the melon into balls with a melon baller.

Fruit Marshmallow
Kebabs

Makes as many as you want

a variety of fresh fruit — grapes, melon cubes,
  kiwifruit, fresh pineapple, strawberries
bamboo skewers
marshmallows
lemon or lime juice to drizzle
mint leaves to garnish

Cut the fruit into 3 cm pieces — not too small
or they will fall off the skewers.

Thread a colourful mixture of fruit pieces on
to each skewer, adding 2 marshmallows to the
mix.

Drizzle with lemon or lime juice and garnish
with mint leaves.

Friends are kind to each other and
cherish each other's hopes and dreams —
why would they suddenly pick on you
and bring out a clipboard
to mark your entertaining efforts
out of 10?

Rhubarb Berry
Oat Crumble

Makes 6

6	thick stalks rhubarb, cut into 2 cm slices
3 cups	mixed berries — strawberries, raspberries, blackberries or blueberries (fresh or frozen)

For the crumble topping

150 g	butter, cut into cubes and softened to room temperature
1 cup	brown sugar, firmly packed
¾ cup	flour
1 cup	wholegrain rolled oats
	icing sugar to dust

Preheat the oven to 180°C. Coat 6 small pudding bowls or ramekins with non-stick baking spray.

Divide the chopped rhubarb and berries between the prepared bowls.

To make the crumble, beat the butter and brown sugar together until fluffy and creamy. Mix in the flour and rolled oats. The mixture will be quite crumbly. Sprinkle the topping over the fruit.

Bake for 40–45 minutes until the fruit is bubbling up through the toasted crumble topping.

Serve warm, dusted with icing sugar and with yoghurt, whipped cream or ice-cream.

Roast Figs with
Blue Cheese

This is more of an idea than a formal recipe.

2	large ripe figs per person, halved lengthwise
	icing sugar to dust
1 large chunk	creamy blue cheese to serve
	wholemeal toast to serve
	yoghurt or softly whipped cream to serve (optional)

Preheat the oven to 200°C.

Lay the halved figs in a shallow ovenproof tray or roasting dish. Sprinkle with a light dusting of icing sugar.

Roast for around 15 minutes until the figs have softened and are just lightly golden. The icing sugar should have caramelised with the fig juices.

Serve with a chunk of soft creamy blue cheese and some wholemeal toast or, if desired, with yoghurt or softly whipped cream.

Raspberry Mousse

Serves 6–8

For the raspberry sauce

1 cup	raspberries (fresh or frozen)
1 tablespoon	water
2 tablespoons	sugar
	icing sugar (if needed)
	lemon juice (if needed)

For the mousse

300 ml	cream
2 tablespoons	icing sugar
1 punnet (about 2 cups)	fresh raspberries
	extra icing sugar to dust

To make the sauce, place the raspberries, water and sugar in a small saucepan over a medium-high heat and bring to the boil. Simmer for 2–3 minutes. Allow to cool, then purée in a blender or food processor. If the sauce is too sour, add some icing sugar; if too sweet, add a squeeze of lemon juice to sharpen the taste. Chill until really cold.

To make the mousse, whip the cream and icing sugar together until the cream is very thick and it holds its shape. Tip the punnet of raspberries into a bowl, reserving some for garnish, and mash with a fork. Gently fold the mashed raspberries into the cream.

Layer the mousse and sauce into glasses and chill in the fridge.

To serve, add the reserved whole berries and dust with the extra icing sugar.

Piped Meringues

Makes 12 large or 36 small

3	egg whites
1 cup	caster sugar

Preheat the oven to 115°C. Line an oven tray with non-stick baking paper.

Beat the egg whites in a metal, china or glass (not plastic) bowl with an electric mixer until thick and frothy. Gradually beat in the castor sugar, a spoonful at a time, until the mixture is thick and glossy. Don't add the sugar too quickly or it won't dissolve properly.

Spoon the mixture into a piping bag fitted with a star nozzle. Pipe swirls of meringue on to the prepared tray, ending with a little peak at the top.

Bake for 45 minutes or a little longer if you have made larger meringues. When the meringues feel dry, crisp and just lift off the paper, they are ready. Cool on a wire rack. These will keep in an airtight container for 3–4 weeks.

Variation — to make the cover recipe, fill store-bought pastry cases with raspberry mousse (see recipe on page 285). Drizzle with the raspberry sauce then top with piped meringues.

Rosewater Pistachio Truffles • Jaffa Fudge Fingers • Honey Spiced Roasted Nuts • Gluten-free Coconut Ice • Hazelnut &

Baileys Chocolate Fudge • Coconut Apricot Chocolate Truffles •
Orange & Raisin Fudge Slice

Rosewater
Pistachio Truffles

Makes 30

¾ cup	shelled pistachio nuts
2½ cups	fine desiccated coconut
400 g can	sweetened condensed milk
1 teaspoon	mixed spice
2 teaspoons	rosewater
½ cup	extra coconut for coating

Preheat the oven to 180°C.

Place the pistachios in a roasting dish and roast for 5 minutes until golden.

Transfer the pistachios to a food processor with the coconut and process until the nuts are roughly chopped. Add the condensed milk, mixed spice and rosewater and process into a sticky paste.

With wet hands, form the mixture into little balls. Then roll the truffles in the ½ cup of coconut to completely coat them.

Store in a covered container in the fridge. They will keep for 2–3 weeks. The truffles freeze well too.

Rosewater is available from the deli section of good supermarkets. It is a clear liquid and is often used in Middle Eastern cooking for such recipes as Turkish Delight.

Taffa Fudge Fingers

Makes 36–40 pieces

2 x 200 g packets	orange chocolate thin biscuits
200 g	butter
¾ cup	caster sugar
2	eggs
¼ cup	cocoa
2 teaspoons	mixed spice
1 teaspoon	cinnamon
½ cup	chopped nuts — walnuts, pecans, hazelnuts, etc, or a mixture
1 cup	sultanas
1 teaspoon	vanilla
	grated rind of 1 orange

For the icing

2½ cups	icing sugar
½ cup	cocoa
30 g	butter, melted
5–6 tablespoons	boiling water

Coat a 20 x 30 cm slice tin with non-stick baking spray, then line it with non-stick baking paper and spray the paper. Process the biscuits to fine crumbs in a food processor.

Melt the butter in a large bowl in the microwave. Stir the sugar and eggs into the melted butter. Microwave for 30 seconds on high, stir and repeat the process until the mixture starts to bubble. Stir in the remaining ingredients, including the biscuit crumbs, until just combined.

Press the fudge mixture into the prepared tin and chill in the fridge until completely cold.

To make the icing, sift the icing sugar and cocoa into a bowl. Add the melted butter and enough boiling water to mix to a smooth consistency. Spread the fudge with the icing. Place in the fridge and when the icing has set, cut into small fingers. They will keep in the fridge for 2–3 weeks.

*Cocoa always needs to be sifted
as it tends to be quite lumpy.*

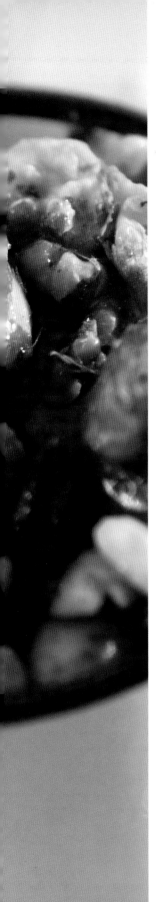

Honey Spiced Roasted Nuts

500 g	mixed nuts — almonds, cashews, walnuts, pecans or peanuts, etc
4 tablespoons	honey
1½ teaspoons	Chinese five-spice powder
½ teaspoon	salt

Preheat the oven to 150°C. Line a large roasting dish with non-stick baking paper.

Place all the ingredients in a medium saucepan and warm over a gentle heat to melt the honey. Mix well.

Spread the nuts over the base of the prepared roasting dish and bake for 20–25 minutes, stirring occasionally, until golden and roasted.

Cool completely before serving. The nuts will crisp as they cool.

Store in an airtight container.

Simple handmade gifts are always
appreciated by friends and family,
and are as much fun to create as
they are a pleasure to receive.

Gluten-free
Coconut Ice

Makes 30–40 pieces

½ can (200 g)	sweetened condensed milk
2 cups	fine desiccated coconut
2 cups	icing sugar
1 teaspoon	vanilla
1 tablespoon	raspberry jelly crystals
1–2 drops	red food colouring
½ cup	extra coconut for coating

Mix the condensed milk, coconut and icing sugar together in a bowl until well combined. Place half the mixture in another bowl. Mix the vanilla into one bowl and the jelly crystals and food colouring into the other.

Place a sheet of non-stick baking paper or a silicone sheet on the bench. Sprinkle it with ¼ cup of the extra coconut. Place the vanilla mixture on the coconut and cover with a second sheet of non-stick baking paper. Roll the mixture out between the sheets into a rectangle 1 cm thick and about the size of an A4 piece of paper. Repeat the process with the raspberry mixture.

Remove the top sheets from both mixtures and gently lay the raspberry rectangle on top of the vanilla rectangle. Press down firmly so they stick together well. Wrap in plastic wrap and refrigerate for an hour.

Cut into small squares to serve. Coconut ice can be stored in an airtight container for 1–2 weeks.

To shell hazelnuts, roast for 4–5 minutes in an oven preheated to 200°C. When the outside skins have darkened, place the nuts in a clean tea towel and rub well. The rubbing will remove the papery skin from the outside of the hazelnut. Don't worry if bits of skin don't get removed.

Hazelnut & Baileys
Chocolate Fudge

Makes 20 pieces

400 g can	sweetened condensed milk
1 teaspoon	coconut essence
220 g	dark chocolate (70% cocoa solids), broken into pieces
2 tablespoons	Baileys liqueur
1 cup	hazelnuts, shelled and chopped

Line a 12 x 20 cm loaf tin with plastic wrap, leaving some overhang.

Place the condensed milk and coconut essence in a saucepan over a medium heat. Stir and bring to a simmer. Simmer for 2–3 minutes, stirring constantly, until the mixture thickens slightly.

Remove from the heat and stir in the chocolate until it melts and the mixture is smooth. Stir in the Baileys and hazelnuts, then pour into the prepared tin. Refrigerate for at least 2 hours or overnight.

Remove the fudge from the tin, using the plastic wrap to lift it out. Cut into squares. Store wrapped in the fridge, or frozen. They will keep for 2–4 weeks.

Variation — you can use this recipe to make yummy truffles, which are great served with coffee. Once the mixture has cooled and firmed up, roll it into balls and freeze. Then dip the balls into dark melted chocolate and place on a tray lined with baking paper until the chocolate sets.

For this recipe to be really successful, you need to make sure the chocolate has a high percentage of cocoa solids — at least 70%. It won't set well with other chocolate.

Coconut Apricot
Chocolate Truffles

Makes 36

1 cup	finely chopped dried apricots
½ cup	fine desiccated coconut
4 tablespoons	sweetened condensed milk
375 g packet	chocolate melts

Line a 20 x 30 cm baking tray with non-stick baking paper.

Mix the apricots, coconut and condensed milk together in a bowl. With wet hands, roll into walnut-sized balls and place on the prepared tray. Place in the freezer for an hour.

Melt the chocolate melts according to the packet instructions. Using a dipping fork, dip the truffles into the melted chocolate and place back on the tray. Don't refrigerate the truffles once they have been dipped as the chocolate can sweat. Store in a cool place. They will keep for 2–3 days.

This recipe freezes well. After the mixture has been rolled into balls, place in the freezer. Dip in the chocolate just before serving, but don't freeze the truffles after they have been dipped as the chocolate will sweat.

Orange & Raisin Fudge Slice

Makes 24–30 pieces

2 packets (around 400 g)	plain or wine biscuits (can be gluten free)
225 g	butter, melted
400 g can	sweetened condensed milk
1½ cups	raisins
	grated rind of 1 orange
1 cup	fine desiccated coconut
For the icing	
2 cups	icing sugar, sifted
50 g	butter, softened
	grated rind of 1 orange
3 tablespoons	orange juice

Coat a 20 x 30 cm slice tin with non-stick baking spray. Line with non-stick baking paper and lightly coat the paper with baking spray.

Place the biscuits in a food processor and process to fine crumbs.

Mix the melted butter, condensed milk, raisins and orange rind together in a bowl. Then add the biscuit crumbs and coconut, and combine well.

Press the mixture into the prepared tin and chill in the fridge until cold.

To make the icing, mix all the ingredients together in a bowl to a smooth consistency.

Spread the icing over the chilled slice and use a fork to make squiggles in the icing.

Store in an airtight container for up to 10 days.

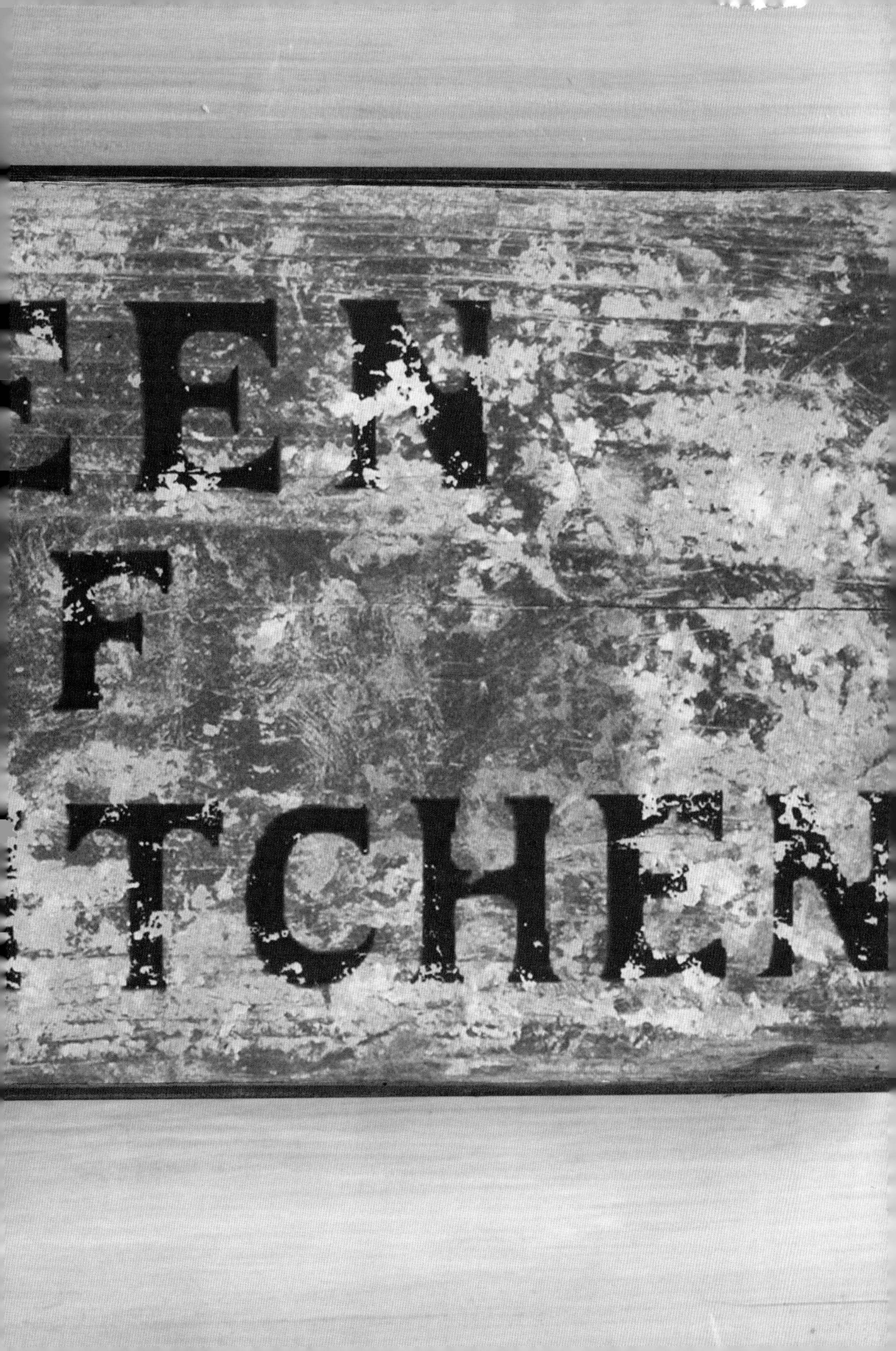
EN
F
TCHEN

Essential
Weights and Measures

Working out the different wordings and quantities in recipes can become a bit of a minefield. Here is a useful list of conversions.

Temperature Conversions

Description	Celsius	Fahrenheit
Cool oven	110°C	225°F
Very low oven	150°C	300°F
Moderate oven	180°C	350°F
Hot oven	220°C	425°F
Very hot oven	230°C	450°F

Liquid Conversions

5 ml	1 teaspoon
15 ml	1 tablespoon
250 ml	1 cup
600 ml	1 pint
1000 ml / 1 litre	1¾ pints

NB: The Australian metric tablespoon measures 20 ml.

Length Conversions

2.5 cm	1 inch
12 cm	4½ inches
20 cm	8 inches
24 cm	9½ inches
30 cm	12 inches

Ingredients

butter	100 g	1 American stick
	225 g	1 cup
	30 g	2 tablespoons
cheese	115 g	1 cup grated tasty
	150 g	1 cup grated Parmesan
egg whites	1 large (size 8) egg white	55 ml or 30 g
flour	150 g	1 cup
golden syrup or honey	350 g	1 cup
onions	1 cup chopped	115 g
rice	200 g	1 cup uncooked rice
	165 g	1 cup cooked rice
sugar	225 g	1 cup caster or granulated sugar
	200 g	1 cup brown sugar
	125 g	1 cup icing sugar

Ingredients' Common Names

aubergine	eggplant
baking paper	parchment paper, silicone paper
cannellini beans	white kidney beans
peppers	capsicums, bell peppers
coriander	cilantro
courgette	zucchini
spring onions	green onions, scallions
fillet (of meat)	tenderloin
icing sugar	confectioners' sugar
rocket	arugula, roquette

Food Label Secrets

Understanding and interpreting food labels is another challenge altogether. Here's a list of key points to help you understand what's in the ready-made food you are buying:

- Ingredients are listed in order of volume from largest to smallest. If the first ingredient is cream, for example, you know that is the main ingredient. A short list usually means the item has fewer artificial ingredients.

- Check out the information about serving size — even quite small packages can have more than one serving.

- To get a quick idea of whether the item is a healthy choice, use the following percentage guidelines per 100 g:

  - more than 10 g of sugar is a lot and a less than 2 g is a low-sugar product
  - more than 20 g of fat is high and less than 3 g is low
  - 5 g of saturated fat is high and less than 1 g is low
  - more than 3 g of fibre is high and less than 0.5 g is low
  - more than 0.5 g of sodium is high and less than 0.1 g is low.

Acknowledgements

I owe a big thank you to all our wonderful staff at Seagars Cook School, Café and Kitchenware Store in Oxford.

I would like to especially thank Deborah O'Neill and Trish Craig for your support and mad dashing about to get props and bits and pieces for the photo shoots. I could not have managed without you.

Thanks to Annie Graham — stylist extraordinaire. A special thanks to fairy god-daughter Claudia Frew for all your help with the photos. Lyn Hunter — a fabulous PA. My publisher, Jenny Hellen at Random House. Maree O'Neill for hair, makeup and general fussing about.

Thanks also to the wonderful folk at the Oxford Farmers Market, the Oxford Museum and the Oxford Art Gallery. Emma's, the fabulous store in Oxford. Richard and Dawn Sparks of Northbrook Colonial Museum for the loan of wonderful old kitchen paraphernalia.

And thanks to Cranfields and Asko stores in Victoria Street, Christchurch. To Forget-me-nots, 22 Conal Street, Woolston, Christchurch; The Painted Room, 804 Colombo Street, Christchurch and to our new Village Green Antiques store in Oxford.

Finally, a huge thank you to Jae Frew. A great friend and a fabulous photographer!

Index